I WISH SOMEONE WOULD HAVE TOLD ME THAT!

Messages to Those Who Come After Me... to Those Searching for Peace and a Fresh Start

"Get all the advice and instruction you can, so you will be wise the rest of your life."

Proverbs 19:20 (NLT)

By Dr. Monique Kammer

I Wish Someone Would Have Told Me That! Messages to Those Who Come After Me…
Trilogy Christian Publishers A Wholly Owned Subsidiary of Trinity Broadcasting Network
2442 Michelle Drive Tustin, CA 92780

For information about special discounts for bulk purchases, please contact Trilogy Christian Publishing.

Manufactured in the United States of America
10 9 8 7 6 5 4 3 2 1
Library of Congress Cataloging-in-Publication Data is available.
ISBN: 978-1-63769-518-0
E-ISBN: 978-1-63769-519-7

Dedication

This book is dedicated to my Heavenly Father, the *One* who has never left nor forsaken me. He has been alongside me, guiding me and His spirit inside me, reassuring me ever since I was a child, baptized at ten years old. He is the light that shines for me when I am lost in the dark and the sun that shines down on me, reminding me of His magnificent glory, mercy, and grace. He sets my mind straight during times of confusion and points me in the right direction, He gives me courage and strength during times of doubt and pain, and He works in me daily, nurturing and maturing me, building me up to do his work.

To Jens, my earthly forever, my husband and biggest fan. Thank you for believing in me; thank you for your constant words of encouragement when I was in doubt. Thank you for reading and rereading and helping me to bring clarity. I love you with all my heart.

To my mother, Martha, my daughter, Roneisha, and my son, Mark. You have been my motivation in life, and you probably didn't even know it. Caring for you is one of my greatest joys. I thank God for you, and I love you dearly.

Introduction

I would have never known that there was scripture in the Bible to offer us guidance, comfort, support, and encouragement for every situation in our life. That in and of itself is the most important thing I wish someone would have told me.

My life has not been easy. In fact, it has been downright difficult in some areas. I have had many hardships starting from a young child. For a long time, I allowed these hardships to shape my life, to form my character, and to be the determining factor in my failures and successes. I was motivated by my hardships, and I was shackled by them as well.

I pray that when you finish reading this book, receiving the messages that I wish someone would have told me, that I can spare you a little bit of heartache. I hope that I can help you take a long hard look in the mirror and embrace who you are by seeing yourself the way our Heavenly Father sees you, as a person worthy of love and acceptance, regardless of your failures.

I pray that by the end of this book, you have created a five-year plan that will help you move toward becoming the person that God intended you to be. Yes, a five-year plan to *move toward* the reason you were created. It takes a while for God to prepare us for His work, for His specific purpose in our life. So, when you stumble, when you fall, and when you come across obstacles, the Book of James says, count it all as joy:

> Consider it nothing but joy, my (b)brothers and sisters, whenever you fall into various trials. Be assured that the testing of your faith [through experience] produces endurance [leading to spiritual maturity and inner peace]. And let endurance have its perfect result and do a thorough work, so that you may be perfect and completely developed [in your faith], lacking in nothing.

James 1:2-4 (AMP)

You are being seasoned for your calling. So, stand up, brush yourself off, and start all over again. It's okay! In fact, it's necessary.

Finally, I pray that your walk with Christ is strengthened as you read this book and are equipped with Scriptures, examples, prayers, and messages to support you in life, messages that I wish someone would have told me.

Table of Contents

Part I: The Pressures of Life

What they said about me mattered. How they said it mattered even more. I would rewind the words and phrases over and over in my mind. I can hear their voices—whomever voice it was, it was everyone's voice. Everyone was right. When they said I was not beautiful, then I was not; I was hideous. When they said I was not smart, then I was not; I was stupid. When they said I was too tall, it was true, I was a girl, taller than most of the boys, and I had huge ghastly feet to match. When they said my skin was too dark, I was unsightly and as black as night. When they said I was too skinny, I was bony and skeletal. Everything they said about me was heightened and magnified in my mind, so when they said I didn't belong, I really believed them, and I embraced ostracism. Oh, the pressures of life at such a young age.

I didn't get angry. That was the last thing I wanted to do. If I became angry at them, wouldn't that just push them further away, leaving me more alone when all I wanted was to fit in? But they didn't see me worthy to fit in. I wasn't like them, any of them, even the ones that seemed to share my resemblance.

I was raised by a mother who loved me and said so. She also did her best to show me. I was told by family members that I was pretty and smart and can do whatever I wanted. So, I was confused about what others said about me and saddened by the way they treated me. This was my childhood. Confused as to who I was. What a contrast between what I learned at home and what I experienced while in the world. Was I pretty, smart, loveable, and empowered to be whatever I wanted to be in life like my family told me? In the beginning, it sure didn't feel that way. How other's saw me was quite different than what I was told by my family. And to be honest, I was around other people more than my family. I was in a school environment for approximately eight hours each day. At 7 a.m. in the morning, I was out the door and on the way to school, returning home around 3 in the afternoon. My brothers and I were latchkey children, with mom returning home after 4 p.m. From 4 p.m. to 8:30 p.m. were homework, baths, dinner, and bed. So, I endured ridicule and ostracism way more than I experienced acceptance and love. I wish someone would have told me that how others see me didn't matter at all. I wish I would have had a more solid foundation of who I really was.

If I had a more solid foundation, I wouldn't have spent so much time searching for acceptance; I would have known that I am perfectly made, and so is everyone else. In fact, no two people are alike, not even twins. I am exactly how I am supposed to be. I wish someone would have told me that my appearance and my path in life is unique and so it should not be compared with another. It would have saved me years of chasing after worthless desires. I would have been able to handle the pressures of life more gracefully.

In fact, if I would have known that I truly had freedom of choice and that I was empowered by the Holy Spirit, my life may have gone quite differently. I could have chosen to process life in a healthier way and tap into the love that truly surrounded me every moment of the day. It really didn't matter what other people thought or said. The only real thing that mattered was what was in my heart, and thus I could have stayed true to my unique self and followed the path that had already been carved out especially for me.

I wish I would have known how strong I was, how empowered I was. I wish I would have known that life will have obstacles and that the strength to get through those obstacles was inside me; all I had to do was to tap into that strength, surrender to it and gain the capacity to overcome all struggles.

Having the power and capacity to overcome the pressures of life makes one resilient. It builds perseverance and character. I wish I would have known to find the joy in the journey of life much sooner—the joy of learning through failures rather than the feelings of shame and persecution for my failures.

And I really wish that I would have known that the only way to live a successful life is to fail. Failure is how we grow. We learn from mistakes, and as long as we have breath, we can start life over and over again. It is my life; I am in charge, and at the end of it all, my life will be exactly what I make it.

"Therefore, preparing your minds for action, and being sober-minded, set your hope fully on the grace that will be brought to you at the revelation of Jesus Christ" (**1 Peter 1:13,** ESV).

I am hoping that by the time you finish Part I of this book, you can start to formulate answers to the questions, who am I? How do others see me? Does it matter? Am I exercising my right to "freedom of choice" in life? Can I embrace where I am right now, or should I start to chart out a course for where I want to be?

I hope that as you read my experiences, you feel empowered to make choices in your life that will place you on the path to live the life you were born to live with confidence and courage. If you have the opportunity, I hope that you encourage your children to embrace their unique selves and do what their heart desires; and I pray that they have established a direct line of communication from their hearts to the Maker of that heart because the path to true happiness and contentment can only come from Him.

Don't wait another moment.

"For I know the *plans* I have for you," declares the LORD, "*plans* to prosper you and not to harm you, *plans* to give you hope and a future" (Jeremiah 29:11, NIV; emphasis added).

Chapter One: Who Am I? How Do Others See Me? Why Does It Matter?

How They See Me...Early Years

I absolutely hated my appearance. As a young child, I was teased for my dark skin and large eyes and often called bug-eyes, tar baby, and ugly. I remember this constant teasing from early elementary. Every time I looked in the mirror was an affirmation of their taunts; they were right; I saw very dark skin and exceptionally large bug eyes; I too saw ugly. The teasing only grew with intensity as I got older. Names were harsher, and even those that had brown skin like mine joined in with the teasing. Unfortunately, in my culture, it is believed that there are degrees of darkness, of course, with the fairest skin being most acceptable, most beautiful; but my skin was of the darkest shade and was seen as ugly or distasteful. It didn't help that I was quite tall in elementary school, and with height comes big feet to match. To round it all out, I was a skinny child. Eventually, I believed that every negative thing that happened to me was because I was a tall, ugly girl with dark skin and bug eyes.

I remember vividly in elementary school being the last person chosen for sports teams. I remember standing there as all the children were called, one after the next. I dreaded being the last person standing because, truly, all eyes were on me, the ugly bug-eyed girl. I distinctly remember a time when no one wanted me on their team; so, the teacher, wanting to get the physical education lesson started, just placed me on a team. The results of her actions were humiliating. The team that received me moaned and groaned while the others laughed and pointed. The teacher simply turned and walked onto the kickball field without a glance in my direction. The teams took their positions, and I walked quietly behind, with the hood of my jacket over my head, sheltering me from the eyes blazing at my ugliness. This was the routine for every physical education lesson where we had to have teams. Wouldn't it have been better to select the teams in a way that was more random, like having students cover their eyes and draw either a number one or number two from a bowl? The ones would be one team, and the twos another? There are plenty of ways to have solved this incident. But unfortunately, the negligence of that adult, and others like her, added to my negative self-perception.

My mother was a multitasker. Working hard and raising my brothers and me on her own. When I was a little girl, she took the time to skillfully sew all my clothes. She placed them on my skinny little body and smiled with satisfaction as I pranced around in my new garments. She made colorful dresses and two pieced pants sets from patterns that matched the current styles. She washed and carefully combed my hair every weekend. She spent time to perfectly part sections of hair, installing little colorful rubber bands and braiding the hair perfectly before placing a colorful barrette at the end. I was her only daughter, and she took her time making me pretty. My uncles spoiled me rotten with words of flattery and lots of hugs and love. I remember one uncle telling me, "the darker the berry, the sweeter its juice." I did not understand that phrase until much later in life. He was complimenting my dark skin. I just knew that when I was with my family, I was a pretty princess, and being the only girl with four brothers, I had an abundance of love and attention. However, that is not what shaped my self-image as our time together as a family was much less than the long days of torture at school. I heard more words of ridicule and hatred than I did of love.

Middle school was worse than elementary. Children are exposed to cruelty and meanness more and more as they grow up, and there was no restraint in hurling the new cruel and insensitive phrases towards me. Middle school was indeed one of the loneliest times of my life. My brothers were making their own friends, and I didn't see them during passing periods. I was also exposed to more children in middle school. Rather than one teacher and one group of students daily like elementary, middle school brought six different teachers with six different combinations of students. The bullies were sprinkled throughout my six periods enough to guarantee that I was teased all day long. I was thankful when the bell rang at the end of sixth period signaling the end of the day.

As time passed, our family kind of grew apart, going their own ways. My beloved uncle moved out of state, and my mother grew increasingly busy raising three boys and a daughter on her own. Her career started to bloom, and she had more responsibility at work. We were latch-key children, letting ourselves in after school and getting busy with homework and household chores. Well, we did not exactly "get busy," but it was done before she came home, most of the time. My support system had dwindled. During elementary years, I learned how to isolate, so being alone was not something new, but the level of humiliation from my peers was certainly new, and sadly, there were more teachers who ignored the abuse; now, I was practically invisible to six adults. I often felt like I was surrounded by people who wanted to hurt me.

Planting a Seed

I would like to plant a seed for you in hopes that you may desire to research and understand systemic oppression.

The lack of care from my teachers as early as elementary was the beginning of systemic oppression for me, a young black female. How did the teachers see me? Why weren't they more diligent in ensuring I was provided a healthy environment to grow and thrive in? Why didn't they protect my innocence, my healthy self-perception?

The treatment I endured as a child in school was com-

pletely unacceptable. No child should be bullied in school, regardless of their circumstances. My mother took her time to ensure I went to school clean, well-fed, rested, and ready to learn. She entrusted me to the system of education, a system parents expect will nurture, protect, and prepare their children for the pressures of life.

But be informed, outside of the home, school is where children develop their initial perspective about self and others, often influenced by their peers and even adults. It is where some start to see themselves as worthy or more worthy, while others develop the feelings of being worthless or without value. In school, as early as elementary is where we begin to develop biases and stereotypes. At home, parents typically try to show children love, ethics, and values; but the power of peer pressure should not be underestimated, especially during this 21st century when everything revolves around social media and technology. The implications of social media on the health and wellbeing of school-aged children can be devastating.

According to the NCHS, Death rates from suicide for children aged ten-fourteen years jumped by 178 percent from 2007 to 2017, and for every suicide among young people, there are at least 100 suicidal attempts. According to (Bullying and Suicide, n.d.), girls between the ages of ten-fourteen are at a higher risk, and Black children are at an even higher risk. Research also shows that many of the students that committed suicide were told to do so by those that are bullying them. I can't express enough how serious conversations about bullying are. If the conversation of bullying ever surfaces, be sure to watch the child for signs of suicidal notions such as depression, withdrawal, trouble sleeping or eating, reckless behavior, making comments about not being able to hand things anymore. Take all threats or talk about suicide seriously. Regardless of where you live, there are hotlines that you can call to get immediate help, such as 1-800-273-TALK (8255).

Now, of course, all children are not cruel, and some teachers did show *a bit* of concern for the suffering I experienced. But the teasing started so early in life and by so many that through the eyes of a child, it literally felt like the world was against me. At such a tender age, I started to feel the pressure of life.

It turned out that having a friend had more of a negative impact on my self-esteem than being alone. Middle school is a time when boys and girls start to see each other quite differently. We know this as adolescence or puberty. The mocking I experienced in elementary school eventually transitioned into invisibleness in middle school. A part of me was happy that I was no longer seen, but the reality is that it allowed me to sink deeper into a state of seclusion, as I watched boys become interested in girls and girls become interested in boys. They chased each other around, giggling and smacking each other lightly. Boys would pull girls' bra straps so the girls would, in return, chase them, and girls secretly wanted their straps pulled! To them, it meant they were being noticed that they were attractive. So, although they huffed and puffed and chased that adolescent boy around to smack him, they did it with an inward or sometimes, an outward grin. When I did find my one or two friends, I was never one of the girls that got their strap pulled. As the boys chased the girls and the girls chased the boys, all fueled by their hormones and ingenuous energy, I was the audience, still alone and still desiring to fit in.

It happened one day that I developed a little crush on an equally shy and reclusive young boy who actually did not tease me. He, too, was often by himself, and I found myself talking to him one day as we sat at the otherwise empty lunch table together. Him on one corner at the very end of the bench, and me at the other far corner. The conversation was simple, but conversation, nonetheless. I started looking forward to lunchtime, and he must also have because we continued to eat our lunch at those far corners for quite some time before we ended up sitting right across from each other. The conversation was less awkward when we were closer. No one seemed to notice us, and I stopped noticing everyone else. He and I rode different busses home from school. We lived at two opposite ends of town. So, we only shared our friendship while we were in school. I begin to enjoy school. I didn't feel so lonely. We even saw each other during passing periods and exchanged greetings and smiles. It was in eighth grade that I started to look at myself in the mirror again. I had forgotten what I looked like, remembering only that it was ugly. Now I could see that I had changed a bit; I recognized that I had, in fact, grown-up, and I was definitely not the same person that I was in elementary school. I started to see myself differently. It wasn't so bad looking in the mirror. It wasn't so bad going to school.

Of course, eighth grade came to an end, and unfortunately, so did our friendship. I went to one high school, and he went to another. But life continued to evolve over summer. I continued to develop and didn't mind as much when I saw myself in the mirror. That positive relationship began to change my life, boost my self-esteem, and make me feel worthy of friendship.

There was another relationship that helped me to see myself in a more positive light during my middle school years. She lived just a couple of streets away from us with her father and younger brother. She went to a different middle school, and we didn't see each other very often because of the routines of the school week. However, during weekends and summer vacations, we developed a bond that we thought was unbreakable. She was my first true friend, and I loved her deeply. I thought she was beautiful. She was of mixed race; her father was black and her mother white. Her complexion was fair, and she had long dark wavy hair. She was a bit shorter than I, and she was slim and dainty. She never made me feel like I was less pretty than she. She never saw my skin as too dark or my eyes too big. In fact, she saw me as I saw her. We were just two giggling girls enjoying our time together. We experimented with make-up and dressing up and relished the experience of becoming teenage girls together. We experienced our first ride on the city bus as we visited the mall in the city. We spent nights at each other's house and became the sister to each other that neither of us had; we were family. She even spent one of those middle school summers with me visiting my grandmother in Florida. It was another positive relationship that helped to prepare me for the next stage of life, high school. We didn't get to go to high school together. In fact, she was taken from her home by the authorities, ripped right from my arms. Even now, I cherish the memories of that friendship. However, in all its beauty, it also brought pain. I felt a sense of abandonment. Like I wasn't worthy of anything good. Memories of loneliness from elementary years surfaced. I was happy to be starting high school in a few weeks, just so I wouldn't feel the hurt from her absence. I was hoping that high school would bring me new friends. I was hoping that they wouldn't see my differences, just as she didn't see my differences. But I was wrong. The two years I spent in high school, yes, it was only two, were just as traumatic as early life. I was still painfully impacted by how others saw me. But it wasn't just my feelings that were hurt. It was no longer just hurtful words taunted by peers and teachers turning a blind eye to abuse. It was much more damaging.

How They See Me...Becoming a Young Adult

The first thing I noticed about high school was all the activities available to participate in. Football, soccer, basketball, swimming, and tennis were some of the sports they offered. There were also elective classes that were actually fun activities! There were classes like cooking, sewing, woodshop, band, journalism, and more! How great it would be to enroll in classes where the activities took all the attention and left little room for bullying and meanness.

There were flyers all around the school announcing tryouts for sports and clubs. I decided to try out for cheerleading. I loved cheerleading. I was a cheerleader for Pop Warner Little League, where my older brother played football for several years, and I was rather good at it. There wasn't much teasing when I went to cheerleading practice because we were surrounded by our parents, who signed us up and expected us to participate in the activity. There, I felt safe with all the parents around, and I really enjoyed being included. I was a natural. I was strong and limber from years of participating in karate classes. I could do the splits in all directions! I had the most elegant and highest kicks on the team. My moves were clean and strong from practicing karate katas. I just knew I would make the high school team! I didn't only want to make the team; I also wanted to be the captain. Maybe when they saw my skills, they would accept me as my middle school friend accepted me. I was so hopeful!

I attended practices all week long and was ready for the big day. No one paid too much attention to me during the week of practice. This was serious business for the girls, and they took it seriously. I didn't notice the coach giving lots of attention to the other girls. I was in my own world, trying to perfect the moves, learn the words and be the best I could be.

On tryout day, I checked in, received my number, and waited eagerly for my turn. I paid no attention to the cliques of girls gathered together, familiar with each other. Those same girls were the ones that got the support from the coach. But that did not bother me; I was good at this sport! I was limber; I jumped high, kicked high, and had mastered all the cheers. I had no worries. I went in with numbers thirteen, fourteen, fifteen, and I was sixteen. I did a fabulous job; I didn't mess up at all. I smiled so hard my cheeks hurt, but I continued to show my pearly white teeth and happy spirit! Some of the girls couldn't do the basic split, and they also messed up on their words. But I was ready. I did a perfect job; both side splits, and when they asked if I could do the middle splits, I happily did them and raised my arms into a strong high V with tight fists and a big smile. That weekend I waited patiently, especially excited on Sunday. It was Sunday night that the cheerleading coaches went to the homes of the girls that made the team and cheer-napped them! The new teams would spend Sunday night together celebrating and go to school the next day with their faces painted and with school color ribbons braided in their ponytails, still wearing their onesies pajamas with their feet covered. I couldn't wait. I went to bed early Sunday night, but I couldn't sleep. I lay there waiting to be cheer-napped. I laid there waiting until the sun rose, and it was time to get up. I wondered to myself if I should get dressed in regular clothes or keep on my pajamas. Ultimately, I decided to pack my PJs in my backpack until I figured out what was going on. Maybe they didn't announce it on the following Monday; maybe it was Friday. I was still sure it would be crystal clear once I arrived at school.

Before we arrived at the gate, I could see commotion at the entrance of the school. There were balloons attached to the gate and a big sign that said congratulations to the 1986-1987 cheer teams! Just moments after that, a school bus pulled up and opened the door, and one after the other girls piled out of the bus. They had their onesie PJs on and their spirit-braided hair. Their faces were decorated, and they all cheered and clapped as other students cheered and clapped for them. I immediately thought it must have been some sort of mistake. Maybe my mom forgot to answer the phone when they tried to notify her that I had made the team. Maybe she didn't hear them when they knocked on the door in the middle of the night. I ran as fast as I could to the gym area where the cheer coach had her office. She saw me coming, looked me square in the eyes, and turned as if she didn't see me. I stopped running and started walking, a little nervous. Did I really not make the team? I knew I did a good job. What could be the mistake? I knocked on the open door of her office. She had her head down as if she didn't see me approaching. She kept her gaze from me and said with a tight mouth, "there is always next year." I stood there bewildered, hurt, and confused, but I didn't say anything. I wanted to feel invisible again. The tears streamed down my face as I walked toward my first-period classroom. I just didn't understand. I tried my best to appear okay but broke my façade when they started announcing the new cheer team over the loudspeaker at the end of the morning announcements.

I told the teacher that I wasn't well and needed to go to the restroom. She said, "suit yourself, but I am marking you absent." I walked right out of the front gate of the school and walked toward home. No one knew I was gone, and no one cared. I skipped school for the rest of the week. Sitting in the nearby park. I learned later that the Varsity and Junior Varsity teams were made up of all the returning cheerleaders from the previous years, along with only four new girls. There was a brand-new freshman team of twelve white ninth graders. The entire high school cheer team had only one child of color. She was a lot like my middle school friend. She was beautiful. She was a mixed child, of black and white with fair skin and long wavy hair.

That was the first time I became aware of blatant racism. I overheard some of the girls during PE whispering that it didn't matter how good I was; I was just too dark-skinned to be on the team. I didn't fit in. I didn't look like them. All the memories of elementary through grade seven flooded my brain, and I cursed myself for being the dark-black, ugly, bug-eyed girl all over again—my image of self-continued to be shaped by my experiences, by how others saw me. There was only one thing that I thought I could do, change.

My Conformity

As a little girl, my mother braided extensions into my hair, and I loved it, but I did not *need* it. Despite me hating the way I looked like a little girl, I never felt like I *needed* hair extensions, that is, until ninth grade. I also didn't think I needed lipstick or mascara. I did enjoy all the pretty smelling soaps, skin softeners, and perfumes my mom bought me from Avon, as she tried to establish in me the healthy practices of hygiene and how a woman should care for herself.

However, after the first few weeks in high school, after not being accepted on the cheer team, knowing I had the skill and dedication to add value to the team further warped my perception of self. If I had the skill, then it had to be the way I looked. The same torment that haunted me in elementary and middle school. The rejection from this popular, sought-after group affirmed my false sense of beauty and what was necessary for me to be accepted. I knew I could not change my dark skin, but I could try to fit in any other way that I could. I became creative with adding hair extensions, and when I would get to school and put on make-up, the long flowing hair and painted face made me feel that I looked a bit more like what was accepted; and I actually felt pretty.

I wasn't teased in high school. After the cheerleading fiasco passed, the year started to progress nicely. More try-outs were coming, but this time it was for the drill team. The drill team would walk behind the school band in parades and perform routines to the band music. They also performed at the high school football games. It was a perfect substitute for cheerleading, although my heart longed to be a part of that group. I was naturally talented and caught on quickly to twirling tall flags and dancing to the band music. The team wasn't exactly organized, and there was no dedicated coach or teacher in the beginning. This group of girls kind of did it all themselves, with minimal support from the band director, whose primary focus was dedicated to the band students. Many of the girls that tried out for cheerleading and didn't make the team also tried for drill team. The skillset was different, not requiring the flexibility and gymnastics of cheerleading. In fact, those that were committed to coming to practice were pretty much on the team.

Every day, I was sure to put on my face and make sure my hair was nice and flowing down my shoulders or in a ponytail that swung back and forth when I performed my drill moves. In my mind, that helped me to be seen by the teacher. I tried really hard to be creative and dedicated to show that I had what it takes to be on that team. Seeing my skill and dedication, the teacher named me as captain of that team, and I worked harder to prove my worth, using my skills to create routines for the band's music. We won several competitions that year, which helped to build my confidence and shape my character. I started to learn about leadership and how to encourage people and work hard to accomplish goals. The team liked me, respected my choices, and depended on me. They gave me purpose. My head, that for years hung exceedingly low in primary years, started to rise. I smiled more and was enjoying school. My aunt became the adult who oversaw the drill team, and my family attended parades and competitions on the weekends.

Had my conformity opened the doors to happiness? Was I really free from the torment that kept me in a shell during my primary years? Not exactly. Remember, I talked about evolution and time passing; well, as time passed, like everyone else, I entered the phase of adolescence, and hormones kicked in. My peers started to get boyfriends, and the time we spent together became less. After practice, when we would sit around and laugh or even do homework together, disappeared, and I would see them sitting in corners with their boyfriends. I longed for that attention. I wasn't teased in high school; I also wasn't noticed, but I did begin to notice boys, and I began to notice the change in my body.

Suddenly, my long synthetic flowing hair and make-up didn't seem like enough. I was at a loss. And I was lonely again. I tried to drag out drill team practices to keep my friends with me as long as possible, but that prompted a downbeat atmosphere during practice. Some girls lost their interest, and some even quit the team. The year ended okay. We got our recognition and received trophies and accolades during the end-of-year reward ceremony. We hugged and said our goodbyes, some promising to connect during the summer, and then the year was over.

I didn't have anyone to really connect with over the summer. My purpose seemed to disappear with the ninth-grade year. There were no more tall-flag routines to create or dances to practice. But I was close to working age, and there was a brand-new Jack in the Box being built close to our house. So, what better time for me to get my first job. I had developed commitment, resilience, and perseverance. I was developing into a compliant, meek, yet productive young lady. I changed myself to fit in, I gave in to the pressures of life and sought new direction on the drill team, and I proved myself worthy as we won competition after competition. I was positive that I could get a job and be great at it! I put in my application and was called the following week.

How He Saw Me

"Lord, have mercy!" I heard this statement behind me and turned to see why the Lord should have mercy. It was a young man making an exclamation. I looked around to see what he was referring to and saw nothing. He smiled a huge grin, showing a mouth full of braces and rubber bands. Seeing my bewilderment, he smacked his lips a couple of times in my direction. I was bending over the counter, reading the employee manual on how to cook hamburgers, cheeseburgers, Jumbo Jacks, and Tacos. His eyes pierced on my backside revealed that I was the reason for his comment. I blushed and hid my face in the book. He couldn't possibly be talking to me, noticing me, finding me attractive? I just kept reading my manual but watched him from the corner of my eyes as he prepped to start cooking on the grill. On this day, I was to study the process of putting together burgers and tacos, but tomorrow he would be the one to train me on the grill and fryers.

I tossed and turned all night, peering through the darkness at the fan whirling around on the ceiling with a big smile on my face. Outside of my little crush in middle school, I hadn't given guys much thought. Yes, I longed for a boyfriend as my friends started to get them towards the end of the year. But somehow, I didn't think I was worthy. I wasn't pretty without my extensions and make-up. I was super skinny, making it hard to see the new curves of womanhood. The character traits that I developed in ninth grade could not be seen on the outside, yet this guy was looking at me with admiration.

When the light appeared through my bedroom window, my eyes saw it coming before the shadow hit the wall. I sat up, mouth aching from smiling with joy most of the night. My shift was not until 10 a.m., but I was up, showered, and dressed by 7. I was giddy with excitement. I took special care with my Avon lotions and perfumes and made sure the flowing hair was extra straight and pretty. I didn't realize that hair would be tucked tight under a net for cooking safety. I walked to work early, arriving an hour before my shift. I sat in the dining room waiting for him to arrive. At 9:30, I could hear music blasting from the parking lot and saw a car driving up with the guy inside. I tried so hard to hide my excitement. I picked up my employee grill manual and turned toward the wall to appear uninterested, but I peeked out the corner of my eye to see when he approached the clock to punch in.

"Mmm, mmm, mmm!" I heard as he walked by. Instantly a smile spread across my face. He noticed me again! So, it wasn't my imagination yesterday! I watched the clock as each minute ticked by as slow as molasses and stood up quickly at 9:55 and walked toward the time clock. I waited with the card in my hand for the clock to strike ten and quickly shoved it into the machine. I turned around slowly, expecting him to be there waiting for me but there was no one there. I searched for the shift manager who would soon perform the introductions. It was on that day, at the age of fourteen and a half, that I met the man who would just one year later be the father of my first-born child. He was eighteen years old and a high school graduate.

Of course, I knew there was something not quite right with me dating a man who had already graduated high school when I was still in the beginning stages of my secondary years. But boy, did it feel great to be seen by this older guy with a car and a job! My tenth-grade year started fabulously! Although I longed to be a cheerleader, I decided against possible humiliation for the second time and committed myself to the role of Drill Team Captain again. Little did I know at the time that my dreams of being a cheerleader would come to fruition on a much higher level, in my future with much more satisfaction. But for now, I happily embraced my leadership position with the drill team and band. This year was no different than the previous year. We started out on the football field with the other athletes of the fall season, performing at games and even performing at pep rallies. We won competitions and made a name for ourselves. As life picked up at school, it also picked up in my new relationship. We were inseparable. My mom absolutely loved his personality, as he kept everyone bent over in laughter with his charisma and charm, so much that I lost my virginity to him. It was one of the worst experiences of my young life. Not beautiful and romantic and perfect as media makes it seem. I was a child giving away a most precious gift. So, a fast message to young readers, wait. Wait until you understand the beauty of that union that God created. Only then will it bring you the true joy that it was intended to bring.

Let's fast forward five months; my mom took me to a doctor's appointment for what we thought was a urinary tract infection. I did, in fact, have a UTI, but we were also stunned to find out that I was five months pregnant! I never missed a menstrual cycle, I was gaining no weight and had no signs of carrying a child, but I was indeed pregnant. We left the doctor's office silently, my mom not yelling or reprimanding me but also far from celebrating. I didn't know what to think. My young mind could not comprehend the drastic changes that would impact my life. Mr. Wonderful accepted the news, as did his mother, whom he lived with at the time. Hearing the news was such an uneventful experience for both our immediate families. The next months went by in a blur. Doctors' appointments were made, establishing medical for myself and a newborn baby consisting of applying and receiving welfare went without a hiccup. It wasn't until I reached month six that I would begin to see the consequences of my action.

The first act of seclusion came from the school I attended. I overheard adults conversing, saying that I would be just another statistic, a high school drop-out and dependent on welfare. I was removed from the high school and taken to a school for pregnant girls; I was isolated again. The drill team captain position that I loved so much, that gave me purpose and happiness, went to another student, and I walked away from public high school, never to enter again, *as a student*. However, before I left Cajon High School, my counselor by the name of Ms. Brown called me to her office. She sat me down and told me that having a baby as a teenager didn't mean my life was over. She looked me square in the face and told me I could still be anything that I desired to be in life. She told me the road would be tough but that there was definitely still a road for me to follow. I really didn't grasp what she was saying at the time. All I knew was that my world was turning upside down and fast. The joy and acceptance I finally started to experience in school were swept away with a signature on a transfer document; me from being an innocent child longing for love and acceptance to me, the innocent child having a child. I was now deemed a statistic. The school for pregnant youth did not really teach the high school curriculum. Classes were about how to care for an infant. Literature was about the phases of pregnancy. The attendance of the students there was poor, girls suffered from morning sickness, lack of motivation, and in all honesty, school was, in fact, quite boring. All the girls were grouped together regardless of age or academic. The ages ranged from middle school to grade twelve. There was a separate part of the school where girls would attend after they gave birth to their child. There was daycare for the babies and regular studies for the mothers. During my short time there, I watched those girls delivering their babies to the daycare and attending regular classes. At lunchtime, they would spend time with their infants while they ate. Some in groups, like they knew each other for a long time. They dressed like regular high school students and giggled and smiled like regular high school students. Looking at them gave me hope which I desperately needed.

When my uncle, who served as a father figure for my brothers and me since the death of my father, discovered that I was pregnant, he was infuriated. He stormed into our home, walked right up to my face, and told me that he would never lift a finger to help me in life. He said, even if I were crawling upon his doorstep, he would not help me, but he would help my child. He then turned and left as quickly as he came. Those words cut to the bone. The intense pain I felt from the rejection by someone I loved and respected so much would later be the fuel I needed to deliver myself from poverty. But, at that moment, I began to spiral down into the depths of depression and sadness that were so familiar. My mom was steadfast. She never showed a moment of disappointment, nor did she ever reject me. She was by my side from the beginning until; well, she still is one of my biggest supporters and cheerleaders. It is great to have the love and acceptance of a parent, especially because, in month seven, Mr. Wonderful was no longer wonderful. In fact, he was downright awful and pretty much absent from the responsibilities, the restrictions, and the expectations that came with preparing for a newborn. As I began this preparation alone, his time and energy were spent securing the next woman in his life.

Now I was challenged with seeing myself as a mother when I was indeed still a child. Fifteen years old, carrying the life of my own child. I felt neither joy nor sadness. I was simply going through the motions, attending doctor's appointments, buying baby clothes, studying for Lamaze classes, and organizing my room for the newborn. The time flew by, as we didn't discover I was pregnant until I was already halfway through the pregnancy.

Childhood, as I knew it came to an abrupt stop. During the seventh month of pregnancy, immense lower abdomen pain revealed a large tumor on my uterus. I was confined to bed rest and was not able to go to the pregnant school. I could no longer climb the stairs to my bedroom, so the living room became my place of belonging. I felt like I was in a bubble. It seemed that time stood still for me while life continued around me and inside me. I gained a lot of weight, topping off at 230 pounds on my five-foot eight-inch frame. Although I was quite large, I felt invisible. When I did go out of the house for appointments, people stared at me. I felt judged. I felt small. I felt insignificant, so I saw myself as such.

On July 25, 1988, I gave birth to a beautiful seven-pound thirteen-ounce little girl. She was perfect in every way. But I had no idea how to really handle her. She was fragile, and it seemed that I would break her. My mother was there to show me that she was, in fact, quite durable and that regardless of her crying, I had to carry on with bathing her and changing her and simply soothe her after the tasks were complete. I started to feel more confident handling her. The more she grew, the sturdier she became. The father and I tried to work it out but with no success. So, I remained a single mother.

But now, the pressures of the world were different. Now, my troubles were not how do I fit in or how do I make friends. It wasn't about if I were pretty or if I looked enough like the others to be noticed, although that would definitely be the obstacle again in life. At that particular stage in my life, I was no longer the priority. I had a child, and my life belonged to her for eighteen mandatory years. So, what would I do with myself to ensure that she was cared for? I had to see myself through completely different lenses, not a child seeking to belong but a young mother seeking to learn how to provide. During this time, another drastic change was happening under the roof of our home. My mother and stepfather were separating. My mother would soon be moving from San Bernardino County, the only home we had ever known, to Orange County, closer to her work, and my older brother and I would stay behind, living in the condo, for just a brief moment, before we too, separated.

We did not remain in that three-bedroom, two-story condo very long. My brother began his young life that took him in one direction, and I began the life of a young single mother. I soon secured my first of several apartments and attempted to put one foot in front of the other to move in the direction of adulthood and responsibility. I sought to finish high school by getting my General Education Diploma. As I began this journey into adulthood, I would face many obstacles that I created for myself. Obstacles stem from the struggle that I had in developing a strong sense of self. I have only shared a fraction of the youthful struggles that shaped my identity. I will doubt myself time and time again throughout my life; my appearance, my talents, and my worth. Hopefully, as you read this story, you will be able to gain some insight on how to avoid some heartache, pain, or stagnation that life may bring your way.

Key Message

I was baptized at a young age, still in elementary school. I was raised going to church every Sunday and even sang in the choir. I knew of a God. But I didn't know God. Parents, it's not enough to just expose your child to the church environment. Start to communicate that there is a bigger love than the love of mom and dad. Have conversations with your child after their Sunday school service and fill in the blanks that may be missing. Children are inquisitive, build off of their curiosity. When they say their prayers, let them know that those are not just words spoken as a ritual every night but that their Father in heaven hears their voice. He loves them, and He is waiting to hear from their little voice every night. Tell them that their voice, thoughts, and feelings matter, and if ever they need an adult for comfort, and there isn't one around, they can silently pray, and their Father in heaven will hear them and soothe them. If we can get children to believe in the Easter Bunny, Santa Claus, and the Tooth Fairy, we can certainly get them to believe in the Lord their Savior.

I wish someone would have told me that God's love and acceptance was the only love and acceptance I needed. I wish I would have understood that I am made in God's image, and that image is beautiful, valuable, powerful, in control, and trustworthy. I could fill up the page with adjectives that describe how beautifully God made me, but the point I want to make is, I never needed to *be* accepted or to change in any way to feel important and valued; for if I am made in his image, and he is perfectly God, so I too, am perfectly Monique.

Early in life, teach your children that they are perfectly made in the image of God. Just as we teach toddlers ABCs and 123's at an early age, we must teach them that God made everyone uniquely different, yet the same. Show them pictures of children their age from different nationalities and express to them that all the children are beautiful because God made them all! Show them laughing and explain that smiles are beautiful and that it feels good to smile and laugh. Then show them tears and sadness and explain that when we cry or show sadness, it's because we don't feel good; we hurt. Explain that hurt is not always physical; it can be a sadness from our heart that makes us cry.

"So God created mankind in his own image, in the image of God he created them; male and female he created them" (Genesis 1:27, NIV).

I wish someone would have told me to be more intentional in telling my children how beautiful and unique they were and what it meant to be made in the image of God. Even though I suffered as a child and, as a result, tried to be a better mom than my fabulous mom, I still failed my children in helping them to develop a strong identity rooted in God's love for them. I wish I would have been more intentional in telling them, you are uniquely, beautifully, and purposefully created in the image of God, and there is no other like *you*! I wish I would have told them that they possess gifts that no one else has because they are exclusive, and there is no one else in this world like them.

We may share talents with others, but every individual puts their own unique twist on that talent; their signature stamp, given by God. So, hear me when I say, don't waste time comparing yourself to others. There simply is no comparison because there are no two people alike. There will always be differences. Not good or bad, not better, or worse…simply different. Embrace your difference; I know it is beautiful because everything that comes from God is beautiful and perfect. There is no need to entertain conformity; when Jesus died for our sins, we were conformed, we were included in the body of Christ if only we believe. Consider yourself a puzzle piece in the body of Christ, already uniquely shaped, colored, textured, and snuggly fit in His image.

REFLECTIONS

If you are questioning yourself in anyway; your skin color, your hair texture, the size of your feet, your height, your weight, your abilities, your intelligence; what could you tell yourself right now? ____________________________

____

____

____

Based on reading my childhood experiences and how it impacted my sense of self, if you have a child that is struggling with their identity, or struggling to fit in, what would you tell them? What words of encouragement do you have? Write them here. ____________________________________

____

____

____

If you are personally struggling with self-image or acceptance, what message do you think God has for you? ___

____

____

____

____

____

What do you want to say to your children to teach them that God made them perfectly and that it doesn't matter what anyone else says about them? ____________________

____

____

____

____

____

Prayer

Heavenly Father, creator of all things, thank You for making me in Your image. Lord, I know that You are good. You are love. You are kind. You are gentle. You are patient. You are forgiving. You are in control. Lord, thank You for also giving me those attributes, so that I may forgive those that may hurt me with negative words or actions. Lord, help me to act with kindness and love, because that is what You would do, and I am made in Your image. Lord, help me to use these attributes when I interact with people. Lord, I know that I am uniquely made, and that Your love and acceptance is all that I need. Lord, help me to remember that daily. Lord, I know that You hate deceitful, bad talking and lies. These are evil ways. Lord, help me dwell in the fruit of the spirit showing love, joy, peace, kindness, and faithfulness, so that my actions may be contagious and cause others to act in the beautiful image that You made us. Father, thank You for making me in Your image. Amen.

These are Scriptures that really speak to my spirit when it comes to my identity. They remind me that I am perfectly made, and they remind me to forgive those that tell me otherwise. Rather than be angered or hurt by them, I should illustrate the character of God.

- When you are feeling doubtful about who you are, think of this Scripture.

  "Surely you know that you are God's temple and that God's Spirit lives *in* you!"

  1 Corinthians 3:16, GNT

- When you hear people speak poorly about one another, remember the two Scriptures bulleted below and understand that God has instructed us on how we should speak about each other. Separate yourself from those who don't live by God's Words. Share this Scripture with anyone you know who may be suffering from verbal abuse.

  "Do not let any unwholesome talk come out of your mouths, but only what is helpful for building others up according to their needs, that it may benefit those who listen"

  Ephesians 4:29, NIV

  "Keep your tongue from speaking evil and your lips from telling lies"

  Psalm 34:13, NLT

- If you are a victim of verbal abuse or oppression, remember how the Lord feels about those who act out of meanness and hatred.

> There are seven things that the LORD hates and cannot tolerate: A proud look, a lying tongue, hands that kill innocent people, a mind that thinks up wicked plans, feet that hurry off to do evil, a witness who tells one lie after another, and someone who stirs up trouble among friends.

Proverbs 6:16 (GNT)

- If someone speaks negatively of you, forgive them. Do not retreat into isolation. Remember what your God says about you, and rather demonstrate the attributes below, and demonstrate God's character.

> "God's Spirit makes us loving, happy, peaceful, patient, kind, good, faithful"

Galatians 5:22, CEV

> So, as God's own chosen people, who are holy [set apart, sanctified for His purpose] and well-beloved [by God Himself], put on a heart of compassion, kindness, humility, gentleness, and patience [which has the power to endure whatever injustice or unpleasantness comes, with good temper]

Colossians 3:12 (AMP)

Summary

Your self-perception and self-worth are established at an incredibly young age. If you see yourself in a negative light, or you have a false sense of self, *dismiss* those thoughts; God made us in His image, and that is beautiful.

If you have children or contribute to the education or care for youth in any way (teacher, social worker, babysitter, etc.), tell them daily how unique they are. Tell them how they are one of a kind and how there is no one on earth like them. Tell them they are worthy and loved and accepted just as they are, and if anyone tells them or shows them otherwise, forgive them, yet separate yourself from their presence. Do not keep their company.

Who you are and how others see you don't really matter at all. When God was creating you, he didn't consult with anyone at all. He is sovereign. He is the supreme authority, the ruler of all things, and he does not make mistakes. He created you to be perfectly you.

Believe in yourself; you know your talents, just as I knew mine when I tried out for the cheerleading team. Trust that you put a unique spend on talents that others may have; don't feel threatened by other's talents. In fact, celebrate their talents with them!

Finally, pay attention to quiet, reserved, detached children and young adults. They may very well be suffering and need positive reassurance in their life. If they isolate, seek to find something to engage them, as we are not intended to live in isolation. Isolation, when one is hurting, will inevitably send one into a downward spiral towards depression, self-hatred and could possibly lead to addiction or, even worst, death.

Dr. Julianne Holt-Lunstad, PhD, who is a professor of psychology, shares her results of a study on loneliness or isolation, discovering that it has health risks similar to smoking fifteen cigarettes a day or similar to having alcohol disease. She went on to say that loneliness or social isolation is twice as harmful to physical and mental health as obesity. Finally, she states, "There is robust evidence that social isolation and loneliness significantly increase the risk for premature mortality, and the magnitude of the risk exceeds that of many leading health indicators."

Sneak Peek

In the next chapter, you will see that although life may have its obstacles, you and I are exactly where we are supposed to be in life. So, there is no need to fret. There is no need for regret. Everything we experience in life can be used as a substance to grow from. Consider the past as seeds planted; in the future, better fruit will be produced by our actions. Good experiences and not-so-good experiences deliver lessons that can be used to continue to catapult us forward in life or perhaps to slow us down for a moment to reflect. At any rate, we are exactly where we are supposed to be.

Chapter Two: I Am Exactly Where I Am Supposed to Be

"'For I know the plans I have for you,' declares the LORD, 'plans to prosper you and not to harm you, plans to give you hope and a future'"

Jeremiah 29:11, NIV

First Time Around

After I had my daughter, I had a plan to be married, have a great career, and provide her a stable life. I have always longed for companionship, and I knew that a family provides the right foundation for raising a child. I wanted to live in a beautiful house in a great neighborhood and provide a sense of security for my child. I wanted to do the right thing.

My desire for these things didn't really drive me as they should have. I was young and free, and life was in front of me. I was still a child, and I thought in childish ways. There was no one at my fingertips to carve out the path I should take. No one to dictate where my time or attention should be. These are the consequences of becoming an adult before your time. So, I did whatever came to mind, and more often than not, if you are seventeen years old without guidance, and a ninth-grade education, nothing constructive comes to mind. My brother was around from time to time, and the baby's father still lingered in my life.

As you know from the previous chapter, the father of my daughter and I did not make it very far as a couple. Although we tried after she was born, we still just could not get it together. I was ridiculously paranoid and convinced that every time he left my presence, it was to be in the presence of another woman. I could no longer trust men. I was abandoned by my uncle, abandoned by the father of the baby, and there were other dark events in my life that helped to indicate that men were untrustworthy. That paranoia I felt led to be quite true, so listen to that inner voice, especially when you know it has justifications for the advice it gives. My time spent with him was in the past. It brought joy to my life, and it was also a very painful and traumatic time. Unfortunately, the impact of that relationship would follow me throughout my life. It would essentially take me many years to stop bringing the pain, feelings of abandonment, inability to trust, and all the other baggage accumulated by men into my future. But life is full of lessons along the journey.

I got my first apartment before I was an adult. It was nestled at the foothills of the San Bernardino Mountains in California. Not far away was a grocery store, laundromat, bus stops, and food shops—everything a single mother needed at her fingertips. I thought I was doing big things. I was living the adult life. I was doing adult things, but my youth and lack of experience had me living on a hamster wheel. I knew that on the first and fifteenth days of the month, I would receive money from the government to support my daughter and me. They also provided me with food coupons, so we always had plenty of food. There was no money left over, but with the modified rent, there was enough to survive. I did this for several months and felt a false sense of success. Isn't that what other adults did pay the rent to provide shelter and put food on the table to provide nourishment? I kept my daughter nice and clean and well-fed and loved, just as my mother had done for me. When I put her down for a nap or bed, I had time for myself.

In my spare time, I wasn't very productive. In fact, I engaged in some unhealthy behavior, and life wasn't going anywhere. Before I was eighteen years old and legal, I became so drunk that I completely lost control of myself. It was a dreadful experience, I became suspicious, frightened, sick, and I was crying hysterically. I couldn't control my emotions, my bodily functions, or my mind. My older brother had to clean me up and put me to bed, cautioning me not to make any sudden moves but to try to sleep still. It was a horrible experience and one that would only happen one other time in my life. My tolerance for alcohol is extremely low, and it didn't take long for me to recognize it was something I could do without.

I clearly wasn't ready to be an adult. But here I was, living this life I had created for myself. As months continued to pass, the vehicle my uncle had given me broke down, and my kitchen was empty of food. I called the baby's father to see if he could take me to get groceries. He promised he would come, and I waited. And waited. And waited. Ultimately, I walked to the market and got all the groceries we needed. It was a little less than a mile, so the walk wasn't the problem. The cart was overflowing with groceries! With no car, I had to push the grocery basket filled with groceries and my toddler back to the apartment. I had no choice; I needed to get my child and the groceries home.

I remembered growing up what homelessness looked like. I would see people in the parks and in the downtown streets of our city, pushing baskets that appeared to contain all they owned. They were trying to make a way for themselves. My heart always hurt for them. I took in a deep breath of astonishment as I unconsciously compared myself to them. Did I look like them? I was indeed trying to make a way for myself and my child. I was instantly embarrassed. I was ashamed. I felt like all eyes were on me again. But I wasn't *just* the dark, bug-eyed girl. I realized that I had caused myself even more humiliation. I did this to me. No one was responsible for my current situation but me. Now, I was that same girl from early childhood, but I was responsible for another life—a single mother, responsible for a life that didn't ask to be brought into this world. Young ladies, looks are deceiving! It is extremely hard to raise a child on your own. From the outside, you see young mothers, and you think, it's not so bad, at least they have someone to love them. But let me tell you from experience, having a child while you are nothing but a child yourself is a recipe for extreme struggle in life, for loneliness as you see others your age engaging in age-appropriate activities, for dependency as you try to become responsible and go to work or school and you need someone to care for your child. Do everything you can to prevent having a child too soon. Mothers, talk to your daughters about abstinence and the beauty of sex as a covenant between man and wife *and* talk to your child about birth control. We tend to avoid the conversation about birth control because we may fear it is condoning their choice to have sex before marriage, but it is better to have your child lose their virginity than to lose their childhood and prematurely start adulthood, coupled with all complexities that follow.

While walking down the street, pushing that grocery basket, I started reflecting on the life I dreamed of for my daughter. I remembered that I wanted to give her the best life. I wanted a career, a family, and to be secure. As the tears flowed down my face and the feelings of guilt engulfed me, telling me that I was a failure as a mom, I saw a black car that looked similar to my daughter's father coming towards me. It was indeed him, coming hours later than promised. He turned the car around and pulled up behind us. I continued walking as another epiphany hit me, showing me that I was dependent on him. I was dependent on those food coupons and checks that came in the mail on the first and fifteenth of the month, and it wasn't even enough to fix my broken car. I wasn't in control. I felt helpless but not hopeless.

I remembered what the teachers were whispering about me when they found out I was pregnant. I didn't realize what it meant to be a statistic at that time, but it all made sense now. My daughter was now a little more than two years old. I hadn't made any growth. In fact, I had started to move backward in life, hanging out, drinking alcohol, and wasting my time.

The grocery store experience was a difficult day for me and a pivotal moment in my life. It was exactly where I needed to be. I often share this story with people when they are feeling stuck in life or feeling helpless. What I like to highlight is that I needed the experiences that I was going through at the time, the discomfort of drunkenness, the humility of helplessness, and dependency. It was that time in life that jolted me and made me feel that there was a plan for my life, and this wasn't it. It was at that time in my life where I vowed to never be dependent on anyone and that I would take advantage of the resources afforded to me so that I can become what I was meant to be.

Moving Forward

Thanks to government assistance, there was a roof secured over our heads. Now I knew that I needed to take the next steps. I needed to figure out how to finish my high school education. I left the pregnant girl's school having only completed the tenth grade, and honestly, I only had a ninth-grade education. The tenth-grade year was a blur of pregnancy, delivery, abandonment, becoming a mother, and becoming an adult. School was a faint memory.

Not knowing where to start, I went back to the high school; it was the place where I left off, so surely the place to begin. I entered the school excited at the possibility of being a student there again. When I told them I wanted to re-enroll, they asked for my mother. For a moment, I was confused. There I was holding the fingers of my own child, and they were asking me for my parent. In my innocence, I did not realize that I was still a minor myself. I told her that I lived alone and that my mom lived in Orange County. That is when she looked down with disgust at my beautiful baby girl, who stood silent and obedient, sucking innocently on her pointer and middle finger. She then smiled disingenuously at my efforts and laid a pamphlet on the counter; and, without another word, turned her attention to the next person at the counter. I stood there for a moment, my heart aching. I didn't know what the pamphlet said until I got outside and regained my composure. I just knew that I had just experienced a moment of blatant cruelty and dismissal, which reminded me of how the cheer coach at the school treated me just a few years before. This was just the beginning of these encounters, I would experience them on a much harsher level throughout my life, and they would ultimately inspire me to become an expert in Social Justice and Education.

Looking through blurry eyes, I could see that the pamphlet had a student on the front of it. He was a black male sitting at a regular student desk with a pencil in his hand. He was looking down at a paper in front of him on the desk. I quickly read the document, and a huge smile spread across my face—adult education school. There was a school in my area for people like me! How about that? I walked to my now repaired old Datsun B210 that was gifted by my uncle and drove back to my apartment to sketch out my plan.

It was there at the Adult Education School that I would obtain my general education diploma and receive the ticket I needed to enter junior college. I looked at the pamphlet and was reminded of my high school counselor Ms. Brown. This was the road she was referring to. This was the road that would still allow me to have a successful life.

Although I missed my eleventh and twelfth-grade year in a typical high school setting, it wasn't too difficult to take the courses and pass the GED exam. The students in the classroom ranged from a few years younger than myself to considerably older than me. No one really mingled together. There was no laughing and joking and hanging out, like high school students. These people were quite serious about being successful in class, so they were equipped with the necessary knowledge to take the big exam. So, it was easy to fit right in and accomplish the goal. There were no pressures to establish friendships or join athletic teams. There was no one looking at me, judging the texture and length of my hair or the color of my skin. During those night sessions, it was all eyes on the instructor and all heads in the books. Being focused was effortless, as there were literally no distractions, and I enjoyed school. The months passed by with ease. I started to feel productive, which energized and motivated me. Three times per week, I would drop my daughter off at her grandmother's house and go straight to class. Before I knew it, the task was complete. All classes were passed, and I was ready to take the exam. It is amazing how being there, amongst people who were determined to do one thing, be successful at obtaining this document, so they can move forward in life, made the task so easy. Surround yourself with like-minded individuals to eliminate all distractions. In the typical high school setting, I was preoccupied with fitting in, with being accepted. In this setting, surrounded by focused adults, was exactly where I was supposed to be.

Although receiving the General Education Diploma wasn't as grand an affair as high school graduation, it was equally rewarding. It felt great to accomplish that task and to be placed in the position to move forward with my education. Closer to my dreams. Some may say it was not the ideal situation, and it certainly wasn't traditional, but it was ideal for me. It was exactly where I needed to be. We shouldn't compare ourselves to others; remember, there is a plan created for your individual life. So, do not be ashamed of where you are in life.

Eventually, I found myself at San Bernardino Valley College. It was a Junior College and the place where I would spend quite a few years of my life, much longer than intended. I discovered that the junior college was very much like the high school in structure. I literally had no idea what it was like. I don't suppose I was in the high school setting long enough to really learn what was *supposed* to happen after high school, and although *going to college* may have been a phrase that was tossed around from the beginning of middle school, it is not something that settles into a student's head until the middle of high school. Consider the different topics that may go with the season of life around middle school. Words like homework, friends, chores, the shopping mall, friends, fitting in, school activities, friends, college, fitting in, friends, career, homework, friends. You get the picture; the words college and career are nestled right in the middle of all the things that really mattered to an adolescent. Being accepted, having friends, and fitting in is top of the list for middle school kids, and it was also top of the list for me.

A cheerleading team! Of course! College has football teams, and where there are football teams, there are cheerleaders. I signed up immediately for tryouts. I had the same familiar excitement that I had in high school, but times ten! I couldn't believe it; I had another opportunity to be a cheerleader! I attended practice with the other young adult women after class. In fact, being a cheerleader gave me college credit towards my associate's degree, who would have thought that doing something I just longed to do would also put me closer to graduating from junior college.

The other girls were friendly and not judgmental at all. They all wanted to make the team, and they were all quite focused on perfecting their skills and helping others to perfect theirs as well. The coach had a kind face with smiling eyes, and kind words came from her mouth. Words of encouragement followed by actions that supported those words. She would stand beside some of the girls that didn't understand the moves or dance steps, and she would demonstrate the proper techniques. She ended each practice seemingly satisfied with her efforts at supporting these young women in their goal to become college cheerleaders. We all gathered around in a big circle at the end, and she asked if there were any questions or misunderstandings. The girls were already starting to form a bond. Some girls that were there the previous year were just as helpful and supportive as the coach. I longed to be like them. I could see clearly that I wanted to be a person that helped to ease others' discomfort rather than be a cause of discomfort. I, too, started to help others who needed support. This came quite easily as I remembered my leadership position as a drill team captain. The coach watched me as I naturally fit into the role as a teacher.

When the results were read out to the twenty-five girls sitting around the coach, my name was one that scored the highest. I was also named as the co-captain to work alongside the captain who was returning from the previous year. I was out of control with joy. I knew I was worthy! I knew I was a good cheerleader! In retrospect, as I reflect on my high school experience of trying out for cheerleading and the results of that situation, I am reminded of God's Word, "Do not be anxious about anything, but in everything by prayer and pleading with thanksgiving let your requests be made known to God" (Philippians 4:6, NASB).

Remember how unhappy I was about not being able to be a cheerleader in high school; in fact, I was quite devastated. I felt like it was something wrong with me. I tried to change to fit in. I went to the coach and tried to understand what I did wrong, even though I knew I was skilled enough to be on the team. I had no idea I would be able to cheer in college with people that were kind and accepting of me exactly how I was; I wish someone would have told me to seek peace with God when I am treated unfairly and things are out of my control. I wish someone would have told me not to internalize the results of unjust or discriminatory situations, as if they are my fault or as if I had done something to deserve the unfair treatment. I wish I would have known to be anxious for nothing. This is not to say that I would not have been sad or disappointed, but I certainly would have been able to process the situation in a much healthier way. The fact is, being on the drill team was exactly where I needed to be. I say again; this does not mean that we should accept being mistreated, ostracized, or discriminated against. In fact, please take the proper and necessary steps to expose all hatred and oppression, and know that God is in control and there is something better coming your way.

College cheerleading wasn't the only blessing God had in store for me in the area of cheerleading. There was more to come. Of course, I didn't know it that time, but the message I want to leave you with is, you are exactly where you are supposed to be in your life. As long as you keep putting one foot in front of the other, always moving forward and trying to do the right thing, even though you may stumble and fall, your life will be full of blessings. The Bible reminds us, "For I know the plans I have for you"—this is the LORD's declaration "plans for your well-being, not for disaster, to give you a future and a hope" (Jeremiah 29:11, CSB).

Getting my cheer uniform and making my cheer box was one of the happiest moments of my young life. The first cheer season went without a flaw. I had the time of my life traveling from game to game with the cheer squad. My family even attended some of the games to watch me cheer on the players.

I was no longer that dark-skinned, bug-eyed little girl. She was nowhere in sight. I wasn't that skinny little girl that didn't fit it. I looked very much like a young woman, and I fit right in! All the weight from pregnancy was lost, and I even ran for Homecoming Queen. I remember putting on my mermaid white dress and tiara and sitting on the back of a convertible Corvette as it followed several other convertibles around the football field with candidates. All the young ladies were waving at the people in stands as if they were celebrities in a parade. I was accompanied by another girl who became a good friend of mine during that season of my life. I was crowned runner-up, not queen, but I sure felt like one as I wore my tiara. I felt beautiful, popular, and like I was exactly where I ought to be.

My first cheer season was definitely a success, and my first semester of college was equally successful. But that success was short-lived. As I entered the second year, I was distracted again, and my priorities were not straight. I would pass enough classes to secure a 2.0-grade point average, keeping me on the cheer team, but I was traveling on a very rocky road. I accompanied the veteran cheerleaders to after-game parties and started to hang out, enjoy socializing, and found myself in another relationship; I was distracted.

While on the cheer team, I was introduced to a person who would serve as my best friend for about eight years in my life. We were truly indivisible. I met her because her boyfriend was the best friend of the guy I was dating. Neither of the guys was in college, although they were of college-age. My new best friend and I had so much in common. We were both the only girl in our family. We both had three brothers. We both lost our fathers at a very young age. We were both mothers at a young age. We understood each other, and we did life together. In fact, it was in that friendship that I found a companion to help me get serious about college. But it wasn't before we experienced devastating tragedy in our young lives.

The guys we were dating were not like us; they were not like-minded individuals. And we know that when you are not surrounded by like-minded individuals, you can become easily distracted. If we weren't hanging out with them, we were worried about where they were, as they too thought having more than one female in their life was necessary, and when they weren't with the other females, they were getting themselves into other trouble. It was during those years that I first experienced physical abuse. I seemed to attract troubled relationships, that to me, were difficult to get out of. Difficult because the one thing that I wanted more than anything was to be loved and accepted. So, I excused poor behavior. Eventually, after an argument and fight that caused me to literally jump from the balcony of a second-story apartment building, I was finished with that relationship. I was behind in school credits and not even able to cheer. I was distracted. He tried to return to my life, and I held my ground. Several weeks later, I was told by my friend that the guy was shot in the head while he was out hanging out with his friends in the middle of the night. I went with my friends to the hospital, where I hugged his mother tightly. We were not very close, but we were familiar with each other, and she was familiar with the hurt he caused me. The doctor's announced that he was brain dead and that there was nothing they could do. When all the family arrived, we gathered around the bed and unplugged the ventilator. We sat there and watched him exhale his last breath. I hurt for his family. But my eyes were opened. The life I was living was not the life for me.

We quickly matured and committed ourselves to be serious about life; we started driving school buses to help get us through college. This job allowed us to work a morning shift taking students to school, go to college faithfully during the mid-day, and then pick up our students (bus route) in the afternoon. We then collected our own kids from daycare and ended our day. It was because we, she and I, decided to do it together that I was successful. We were each other's accountability partners. Once we decided to get serious about life and commit to making a better life for our children, there was no stopping us.

I smile when I think back on our first plan to taking control of our lives. We planned to become California Highway Patrolwomen. We both took the written exam, passed it, and moved into the next stage, the physical exam. We worked hard to train our bodies and build our stamina in order to be successful, and we were, in fact, successful on that exam too. We were completely dedicated. But there were other life circumstances, or shall I say consequences, that prohibited us from following that plan. I was told personally to clean up all things on my credit. As a young mom starting life in survival mode, there was quite a bit of damage to my credit. I had no clue about things such as credit. In order to fix the credit, I needed a successful job and, wasn't I seeking a successful job? Wasn't that why I was going through this entire process? It was clear that was not the road I was supposed to travel, so it came to an abrupt halt.

However, we didn't stand still. We continued to put one foot in front of the other. We dove headfirst into becoming educators, she, majoring in Special Education, and me, English Literature and Composition. We were side-by-side as we worked to get our Associate Degree. After securing that degree, we were hooked. We went on for our bachelor's and master's degrees as well, and ultimately both received doctorate degrees.

Unfortunately, we didn't remain the best of friends, separating after the Bachelors's, but we were best friends when we needed to be. As I look back on that time in my life, I am so thankful to have had her during those exceedingly difficult and confusing youthful years. She understood my struggles as they were quite similar to hers. A message to those who feel alone, find someone moving in the same direction as you and do life together. Just keep in mind, people come into our lives for a reason, a season, or a lifetime. So, don't hold on so tightly. This is a lesson I would learn from more than one experience in my life's journey. Holding on too tightly to people can be very painful.

Our separation was a devastating event in my life. We had certainly grown apart over the years as we graduated college, left driving school busing, and began our career as educators. She left California to move to another state, but that wasn't the painful part. I was to visit her in her new town. I was looking forward to that trip, as I genuinely loved her and was closer to her than any other person on the planet. She was part of my family. My family embraced her. In fact, even now, over twenty-five years later, a picture of her two oldest children has a place in my mother's living room, along with my mother's other thirty-four grandchildren. We knew each other's deepest secrets; I thought we would be friends for life. But as the day neared for me to go visit her, I received a phone call from her. She told me there was no need for me to come. That we were just not close like that anymore, for a moment, I couldn't breathe. I was confused. I was hurt and, in a way, although I was an adult, with my own children, I was alone. Again. Abandoned. Discarded. As you read in Chapter One, the only thing I desired growing up was to have a friend that absolutely loved me and accepted me. So, when I was blessed with her companionship, I held on fast. I had no idea that it would bring about the familiar hurt of childhood and leave a scar that would remain for years to come. But during those years that we spent together, I was exactly where I was supposed to be. Her presence in my life served its purpose. The biggest problem was; I just didn't know how to let go. Not of her physical presence, as we had truly not "hung out" since before we got serious about life, but boy did we hang out! It was the pain of abandonment. I thought those types of friendships lasted forever. The friendships where you know their deep secrets, and they know yours. The friendships where you experience life together. The friendships that cause other people to question you when you are by yourself because normally, you are glued to each other's side. I wish I would have known how to deal with the pain of losing that friendship. I wish it hadn't caused me to question myself again. I wish I would have known; friends enter your life for a season, a reason, or a lifetime. It is not just boyfriends that break your heart. Clearly, her time in my life was for a reason; she was my accountability partner for the beginning stages of my becoming a mature young woman. We did it together, and for that, I am thankful.

Blessings in Disguise

I had other blessings during college days; so many things were in my favor that I didn't recognize until I got much older. One of those things was government assistance. It's hard being a single mother, especially when you are just a child yourself. Or perhaps if you just don't know how to access the resources that may be available to you so that you can help yourself. While I went to college, I was given childcare from the welfare system. It was one of the best blessings I have ever had. It allowed me to drop off my children at 6 a.m. and pick them up at 6 p.m. That liberty allowed me to drive my bus route during the day and go to school during the mid-day. On days that I didn't go to college during the mid-day, I took extra work at the bus yard doing kindergarten runs. After picking up kindergarten students from their bus stops and dropping them off at their schools, I would then take the bus early to my afternoon run and sit in the bus and do my studying until school dismissed. As I sat parked in the school bus loading zone doing my schoolwork, school employees would often see me and greet me and sometimes have a conversation. We eventually developed relationships. Some of them asked what I was studying, and I told them I was studying to become a teacher. Several principals said they would keep in mind that I wanted to become a teacher, as they could clearly see my ability to drive a busload of over fifty students while maintaining a safe and orderly environment. I didn't give it much thought, as I still had a way to go. First graduating with my bachelor's then enrolling in the teacher training program. I wouldn't be ready to start teaching for another four or five years, but let me tell you, I was in the right place, at the right time!

Sometimes God is lining up blessings in our life distinctly, and we are in one of three mindsets; the first one I like to refer to as moving at high speeds, so fast we often miss out on blessings. The other is moving in circles, like a hamster on its wheel, because it's comfortable to do the same things; it is familiar and easy, so we do the minimum. We settle even if it gets us nowhere in life. The last mindset is the one where you naturally grow out of enjoying certain activities, being around certain company, or you have maximized a position, and it no longer is fruitful. I call this putting one foot in front of the other, moving in the right direction. I am reminded of 2 Corinthians 9:6 (ESV), which says, "The point is this: whoever sows sparingly will also reap sparingly, and whoever sows bountifully will also reap bountifully." Where are you on your journey? Moving fast, spinning in circles, or putting one foot in front of the other, moving in the right direction?

Try not to be so preoccupied with going after what you want that you zoom right by or delay your blessings. Put one foot in front of the other with just enough momentum that you will not become overwhelmed with life. When we become overwhelmed, there is a possibility of shutting down and only doing the bare minimum. I wanted to be comfortable in life, I wanted to want for nothing, and I wanted this comfort *now.* I did not even consider that as a brand-new Highway Patrol officer; I would not get the favored work shift. I would get a shift that would take me away from my daughter during a time when I needed to be present. I have a sensitive and forgiving soul, yet I was signing up for a career that required me to always enforce the law; there are no gray areas. It was not a profession that fit my personality at all.

Deep in my soul, I knew I needed to go to school. I knew I wanted to put myself in a position to give back to people, to encourage people as my counselor Mrs. Brown encouraged me. But becoming a California Highway Patrol officer would have provided a nice salary for me to raise my daughter, with only a year of training time. I wanted to get there fast! So, I tried to ignore the small voice in my head that said, go to school. I put off school and put all my energy into training to become an officer. But that wasn't the route I was supposed to take, and those endeavors did not come to fruition. The good thing was, I didn't get overwhelmed with the negative emotions that could have come from the rejection of the CHP program and hop on the hamster wheel. I didn't freeze; I knew I was destined for more. Although I wasn't honoring God with my life the way I should have been at the time, there was still the small voice in my head that said, you will do good things in life. He had a plan for my life. So, I committed to going to school.

We live in a world of right now or nothing. We often miss the middle ground; the slow and steady wins the race path. The one that tells us not to become tired or discouraged of doing good, of doing the right thing, *regardless* of how long it takes. If we keep moving forward, and we do not give up, the time will come when our effort provides us great reward for our dedication.

When I graduated with my bachelor's and enrolled in the teaching program, I was told that I could start teaching right away; I didn't have to wait for the teaching credential to be completed. I could begin teaching on an Emergency Credential while I completed the clear credential process. I put in an application in the same district where I was driving the school bus. I learned that several principals wanted me as a teacher in their school; simply because I had been in the right place at the right time. Driving a school bus, developing classroom management skills, communicating with parents, understanding the structure of the school building and the educations system. I already had skills that I could add to my resume before I ever became a teacher. I had no idea that by being obedient, listening to the still small voice, and putting one foot in front of the other, moving in the right directions, I would be blessed continuously.

I became an eighth-grade English teacher at the same middle school my brothers and I attended, the same middle school my own daughter attended. Without knowing, I served those children with the heart of God. I was so full of love and care, and I poured it out on them. They were all so uniquely lovely to me. I could almost see into their little souls. I saw some that needed the nurturing of a mother, some that needed personal encouragement, some that needed affirmation, and some that needed acceptance. I easily gave them all that they needed, and it was easy to do. I was made for teaching. I can sometimes see the little dark-skinned bug-eyed girl in many of them, and I was dedicated to giving them what she didn't get.

Key Message

I wish someone would have told me that once you enter the world of adulthood, time is one of the most precious commodities in life. It is not something we can reclaim. When it is gone, it is gone. So, make the best use of your time. I wish someone would have shared that as long as I put one foot in front of the other, moving in the right direction, working hard at what I am doing, that I am exactly where I am supposed to be in my life. But, if I become idle, wasting my time in fruitless follies, I would suffer the consequences of my lack of productive action. I wish someone would have told me that settling for the absolute minimum to survive will cause me to remain on the hamster wheel of life, making no progress. Accepting the bare minimum, or leaning on others for too long to survive, does not allow me to prepare for obstacles in my life.

Parents, make sure that your children can connect success in life, being prepared for obstacles, with having an education. That is not to say that going to a major college or university is for everyone. However, being in an environment that causes you to grow intellectually, emotionally, and worldly is critical, be it college, military, trade school, volunteering, or family business. Start teaching children early what it means to "work" towards being successful so that they can easily connect education (learning) with being independent. I confess, as a former educator, I believe college is for everyone; however, I am well aware of some extremely successful people who did not take that path. I want to highlight the word successful and capitalize on the fact that in order to be successful, you must put one foot in front of the other, moving in the right direction and learning along the way. It is practically impossible that one is successful without putting forth effort.

It is also much easier to be successful if you find someone to "do life with." When we find others that are moving in the same direction as we are, try to establish a relationship and accountability partner. Find someone who understands where you are trying to get to, and more importantly, one who knows where you came from. Ideally, they would be able to empathize with you because they have had similar experiences. It is then that you can truly push each other. But be careful to hold this person loosely.

I wish someone would have told me that friends enter our lives for a season, reason, or lifetime. It is so important that we know how to handle the unexpected separation of someone who means a lot to us. I like how the Bible uses the parable of salt. Put shortly, salt is a great thing, but if it loses its ability to provide flavor, what purpose does it serve? If indeed the relationship does not continue to produce fruit for you, or you for it, don't struggle to hold on to it. If a person is unfulfilled, find peace in your hearts and go your separate ways. It is this task of finding peace that I have struggled with. But it is knowing that I have God with me forever that has brought me peace.

Some things are simply out of our control. Don't beat yourself up if things don't go the way you want them to go. There may be good or better coming your way. You may be chasing a career, a promotion, or acceptance into a program. You may exhaust yourself do all the leg-work to ensure that you are the right candidate, yet your efforts may be in vain. Know that although that is not the door for you, if you follow the Lord with all your heart and strength and trust in Him, there is a door open for you that cannot be closed by anyone; just keep putting one foot in front of the other, moving in the right direction. As long as you do that throughout your life, you will be exactly where you are supposed to be.

Have you ever wanted something so bad in life that didn't come to fruition, yet you were blessed with it later in life? As you ponder your life and consider my experience with cheerleading, what can we learn? Write it down, so you are sure not to make same mistakes. ________________

____

____

____

What message can you give to your children, or advice to yourself about time being a precious commodity and the importance of always putting one foot in front of the other moving in the right direction? ________________________

____

____

____

Friends come into our lives for a reason, a season, or a lifetime. Have you experienced the unexpected loss of a friend? How did you deal with it, and what advice would you offer to your child about holding friends loosely?

Prayer

My Precious Lord and Healer of my soul, I know that You are all I need, Lord. I know that You are my best friend, my teacher, my motivator and my disciplinarian. I know I have constant access to You-by-Your Holy Spirit which lives within me. Lord, I know that when I call on You, that You hear my cries. Lord, I know You are a God of mercy and grace. You see me when I fall and pick me up again and place my feet back on solid ground. I thank You, Father, for Your forgiveness when I sin and fail, when I do things that disappoint You, when I go against what is good. Thank You for Your faithfulness and showing me a better way to live, a virtuous path to follow. Thank You for closing doors that I should not walk through, although in my ignorance I may be sad, angry, or disappointed. Yet teach me perseverance during these trials, giving me the energy, mercy, and motivation to rise up and place one foot in front of the other, moving in the right directions, Lord, I know that If I do that I will always be exactly where I am supposed to be in my life. Lord, I know You have a plan for my life, may I always seek Your face when I am making decisions. Might I remember to be still enough to hear Your voice, and may I not be overly concerned when I stumble and make mistakes. God, You are there to catch me when I fall and place me back on the path to continued growth and righteousness and leaving childish ways behind me. Thank You for Your provisions. In Jesus' name, Amen.

These are Scriptures that really speak to my spirit when it comes to the faithfulness of the Father, meeting me where I am. They remind me I am never alone, and they remind me to continue to seek Your guidance in my life, for You have a plan for me. Finally, they teach me to grow and not be stagnant, always putting one foot in front of the other, striving for righteousness, leaving foolishness behind me. I should always aim to illustrate the character of God.

- When you are not motivated and you are on the hamster wheel of life, be reminded of these four Scriptures.

> "For I know the plans I have for you," declares the LORD, "plans to prosper you and not to harm you, plans to give you hope and a future"

Jeremiah 29:11, NIV

> "Your eyes saw me when I was formless; all my days were written in your book and planned before a single one of them began"

Psalm 139:16, CSB

> "Laziness puts one to sleep, and an idle person will go hungry"

Proverbs 19:15, ISV

> "When I was a child, my speech, feelings, and thinking were all those of a child; now that I am an adult, I have no more use for childish ways"

1 Corinthians 13:11, GNT

- When friendships or experiences have served their purpose in your life, remember this parable. "Salt is good; but if it loses its saltiness, how can you make it salty again? Have the salt of friendship among yourselves and live in peace with one another" (Mark 9:50, GNT).

- When you've given 100 percent and exhausting all efforts, and things still don't go your way.

> "I know everything you have done. And I have placed before you an open door no one can close. You were not very strong, but you obeyed my message and did not deny you are my followers"
>
> **Revelation 3:8, CEV**

- When you feel you are alone, and there is no one listening."Blessed be the LORD, Because He has heard the sound of my pleading" (Psalm 28:6, NASB).

- When you have stayed the course, as long and tedious as it was, and your need affirmation. "And in Your majesty ride on victoriously, For the cause of truth, humility, and righteousness; Let Your right hand teach You awesome things" (Psalm 45:4, NASB).

Summary

You are exactly where you are supposed to be in life. You, and only you, have the power to control the outcome of your life, even though it may not seem so at times. The ultimate outcome is in your hands. We all have plans specifically for our lives. The Lord says that He knew us before we were formed in our mother's womb and that all our days were written before we took our first breath. And if this is so, and we know our God is good and only good comes from Him, then we can be certain that we are created for a great purpose. The problem is that we tend to get in our own way. Whether we are moving too fast, whether we are overwhelmed by the responsibility of life, whether we have experienced trauma as a child, or whether we are easily distracted, we are the ones in control.

When I first got my apartment and tasted adulthood, I lost focus. I started to hang out and drink alcohol. Two years of unproductive life went by. I was on a temporary hamster wheel until I was jolted back into character, the character that seeks growth and righteousness. But that jolt, too, was short-lived. We are so easily tempted by the *fun* of life (sin), especially when we are not around people that are focused on being good and righteous. When we are committed to growth, we must always surround ourselves with those that are like-minded. Although we may become frustrated with where we are, all the phases of life that we experience are necessary for our growth. We may become temporarily distracted, but if you are a child of God, even if you have backslid, you will feel the jolt that is meant to put you back on track. So be aware and be responsive. The jolt can come in different forms. It can be rejection; it can be death; it can be an accident, a sickness, or even a dream.

I was distracted from my life's plan when I was presented with a faster way to success. I forgot about the still small voice that said go to school, become an educator, and help other marginalized children. I attempted to travel a different path. I put all my time and energy into becoming an officer, approximately a year of my life. In the end, that target I was chasing, that fast road to success, never came into my reach. That rejection from the program was my jolt. But I was responsive, I listened to that voice that was still in my head guiding me, and I obeyed. The path became clear. Doors opened and allowed me to work and go to school with hardly any barriers. In fact, I had a partner to "do life with" to help keep me accountable. I was also blessed with establishing relationships with school leaders, which led to a teaching position in one of the schools. When I put one foot in front of the other, moving in the right directions, not only did doors began to open for me, but I was also filled with happiness, fulfillment, and a desire to do more for people.

Sneak Peek

I am so thankful for the opportunities in life to do better. I am so thankful that it is proven by putting one foot in front of the other, I can progress. I am thankful to know that as long as I am putting one foot in front of the other, I am exactly where I am supposed to be in life. And how fabulous that I get to do life at my own pace, praise God. I am so happy that I have learned that my life is mine and that I have the freedom to choose the path I travel on. In Chapter Three, I will talk about the freedom and limitations of the freedom of choice.

Chapter Three: Freedom of Choice

Eighteen years old! Woohoo! Let's celebrate! Most of us can't wait to be eighteen years old. Before the day ends on our seventeenth birthday, we are already planning what to do when we turn eighteen! In fact, do we even remember turning seventeen? Seventeen is one of those insignificant numbers stuck between sweet sixteen and the fabulous age of adulthood, eighteen.

Because I have spent over twenty years working in public education and planned many graduations, I clearly remember the chatter of graduates (typically seventeen or eighteen years old) looking forward to leaving their parents' home, going to college, or getting a job so they can have their own money, buy their own car, go where they want to go, and do what they want to do.

The transition from adolescence to legal adulthood is such an important time in our lives as individuals, as well as for parents. I have two adult children, a son and a daughter. I have experienced the transition twice, on very separate occasions, because my kids are seven years apart. I remember all the splendor and all the heartbreak. It's fabulous to watch your children grow up and get excited about life, and it's equally hard to watch them go.

When we have our children close together in age, it seems like the transition experience from adolescence to adulthood is non-stop, one big, long, drawn-out activity; so our hearts are a bit more seasoned. Not just in the big transition, in everything! Consider my brothers and me. We are four children, with the first three being back-to-back, but mom had a bit of a rest time before the last child, who came almost five years later. One of us learned how to ride a bike, then immediately the next one, then the next one. My mom was buying those first bicycles with removable training wheels three years in a row! She had to buy three because the training wheels were removed, and then we had our instant big kid bikes, so we all needed our own. It really is bittersweet. When I am asked was it difficult to have my children so spread apart, I tell people that I was happy that my children kind of had me to themselves during those critical years. With seven years in between, they really could get my personal attention, but my heart was also broken two distinct times. There was plenty of time to heal in between. There was also plenty of time for me to forget important lessons learned from the first experience. Moms, I am not saying you didn't experience the same heartache every time a child graduated and became an adult or crossed different *rite of passage* or milestone in life; I am only saying when it happens back to back, it seems as if it is a little easier to deal with.

At any rate, eighteen years of age in the country where I am from is a rite of passage, from adolescence to adulthood; from dependent to independent, from being tried as a juvenile to being tried as an adult. I use the example of being tried as a juvenile and tried as an adult to highlight the responsibility that accompanies that rite of passage. Different responsibilities come with the decisions we make as adults. But isn't it awesome to be able to make our own decisions in life? Isn't it awesome to have freedom of choice?

There is a lot of debate about the phrase of freedom of choice, and as a woman of color and a social justice advocate, I want to proclaim that I agree that the word "freedom" is highly controversial and can be interpreted differently by different people, however in this context, I am referring to the general rights that are granted to a person once they turn eighteen years of age in the United States. So, to make it even more clear, let's say freedom from the constraints of your parents, and thus, ownership of your individual actions.

For me, because I had a child early, it was the innocent of age sixteen that granted me freedom of choice. I guess, sadly, I was making big decisions even earlier than sixteen. For example, the decision that I made that granted me the right to make decisions at sixteen! That decision, having sex and getting pregnant. Do I regret my choice, no I don't? That choice was the start of making me who I am today. But if I had the chance to do it differently, would I? Absolutely! I am saying this with loads of experience to back up that decision, hence this book, *I Wish Someone Would Have Told Me*.... Hopefully, I can help support you with some big choices that you may be faced with.

Indeed, we have the freedom to choose, to make our own choices. From those choices come consequences, obligations, and the determination of how the pavement on the road we are to follow in life will be, rocky or smooth. In fact, each choice we make helps to create the rough gravel, twisty turns, hard hills, and smooth valleys that we travel throughout life. Regardless of anything, life comes with good and bad, but we have more power than we think to make the journey as smooth as possible.

We already know that I passionately believe that we are *always* exactly where we are supposed to be in life, as stated in the last chapter. I say that to give you the utmost affirmation on the choices that you have already made in life. Although some choices we make do not present the results we desire, it doesn't mean that we made a "bad" choice. It only means that the consequences and obligations stemming from that choice are different than expected. Even if it wasn't the ideal choice, I can guarantee that there was something that you learned from that choice. Perhaps something you would not have known or learned in life otherwise. My husband always tells me that the decisions we make are, by default, the correct ones, because it is what we think is most suitable at the time, or we wouldn't have made them!

I want to share some of the choices I made and the things that I learned from them. I want to share the consequences, obligations, and how the choices paved the roads of my life. I want to share them because perhaps you will be able to learn something from my experiences that may help you chose differently, or perhaps it will help you to deal better with a situation that you may be in. I want to talk about these three experiences that I have gone through. Then I want to share with you a recipe for making decisions that you can use in life; on practically any choice you make. The three choices I want to share with you are:

1. The decision to have a baby at fifteen years old.
2. The decision to tell someone when you have been physically or sexually abused.
3. The decision to pursue an education.

A Baby Having a Baby

Now there are two big decisions that I made in having a baby while still a child myself. The first one was to have sex before I was ready. The second one was, having the baby. The second choice may make some people gasp, but the truth is, there is a choice that can be made here as well. In fact, it is where the Freedom of Choice Act comes from. I am not stating that I am against it or for it; I am simply stating the fact that choosing to go through with a pregnancy is a choice and that it is a big choice with even bigger responsibilities. As a Christian, I encourage adoption if you feel you are not in a position to raise your child.

I had no clue whatsoever as to what I was getting myself into for both decisions mentioned. So, going into the situation, I was at a disadvantage. In addition, I was already so ladened with scars from childhood that the scars did more of the decision-making than my brain did.

When your childhood creates scars that aren't properly addressed and which you haven't healed from, it can leave you vulnerable. There are all types of scars that can happen during your childhood, be they physical, mental, spiritual, or emotional hurt. Scars represent an encounter where we were injured, and the simple fact that we have them means we are victorious. Everyone has scars! Don't think you are alone. The scars that we have are accompanied by emotions such as fear, humiliation, dishonor, criticism, guilt, hatred, distrust, abandonment, and I can continue to name emotions you may feel. You are also not alone here.

My decision to have sex was scary. I have a history of sexual abuse, so I wasn't really sure what was supposed to happen when you engage in intimacy with someone you actually care about. Again, I was taking actions and choosing to engage in an activity where I was not properly educated. But my childhood scars of constant humiliation, abandonment, and fear had increased the intensity of my need for love and acceptance. To me, all I could think of at the time was that people who make love, love each other, right? The answer is yes, they do. But let me write that sentence once more. Those who make love, love each other. We first have to know *exactly* what loving each other means in order for the act of sex to be considered "making love." I am talking about the love that God intended for man and woman. This is not a love we understand when we are children. It's a very different love that you feel for your parents, siblings, other relatives, or friends. If you don't understand the depth of this love, you are simply giving a very precious piece of your body and soul away through the act of sex. And once you do it, you cannot get it back. So, I am telling you what I didn't know. Wait! Understand the type of love a man and woman should have towards each other. If you are a minor, I guarantee you, your understanding is not accurate, simply because you haven't experienced life enough to know what it is.

Love between a man and a woman is mature, and maturity comes with age and experience. How do I know? Well, the maturity of genuine love is evident by the choice to *wait* until you are unified in the eyes of God before you share your bodies with each other. I know it's mature because this conversation never surfaced between me and the baby's father. We lacked maturity and self-control; we were driven simply by feelings. For me, the feeling was a desperate need for acceptance; for him, the feelings were hormonal. We didn't have a shared understanding of the activity that we were engaging in symbolized.

In the Bible, it tells us that making love is a good thing and is expected between a man and his wife, two people of the same accord. The book of Genesis 2:24 (ESV) says, "therefore a man shall leave his father and his mother and hold fast to his wife, and they shall become one flesh." This Scripture goes beyond physically becoming one flesh during the act of making love, but also becoming one emotionally, literally bound together as one, till death do you part, all for the glory of God. In fact, as husband and wife, it is the *only* time sex is appropriate; any other time is a sin against God. First Corinthians 6:18 (ESV) says, "Flee from sexual immorality. Every other sin a person commits is outside the body, but the sexually immoral person sins against his own body." If we believe in Christ, our body is the temple of the Holy Spirit; to sin against our own body is to sin against God.

The choice I made to have sex was instantly regretted. It wasn't pleasant, it was painful, and the fulfillment I thought would come after the act did not come! Him being almost four years older than me almost certainly felt different. Again, I ask you to wait, understand the act you are engaging in and the consequences of your actions! Know that once you give this honor to another person, it can never be taken back, and how beautiful it is to be able to give yourself to your spouse, pure and without sexual blemish.

I will tell you when sex is had outside of marriage, it does not bring about the satisfaction and fulfillment that it is meant to deliver. I think this is why, when we have sex out of marriage, we keep pursuing it over and over again, and often from different people, looking for an expected satisfaction that can only come when you make love inside the union of marriage, with the knowledge and maturity in which it requires.

Although I regret that decision, that I am thankful for my daughter, it was such an unpleasant, unfulfilling experience that I didn't do it again for some time. Unfortunately, it only takes that one time to become pregnant. I had literally forgotten all about the experience. About four-five months later, I complained of pain when urinating. When my mother took me to the doctor expecting me to have a bladder infection, she was right, I definitely had a urinary tract infection, but that news was accompanied by the fact that I was also with a child. I was completely dumbfounded. How can something I did one time several weeks before surface right now! Was that possible? I still had monthly periods! Again, I warn you, be incredibly careful what you get yourself into. Understand the act as well as the consequences of your actions. I know it's a sensitive subject, but parents, educate your children.

I was already past the first trimester when we discovered I was pregnant. Not having the baby was never a discussion for me. When a family member brought up the idea, I was confused. I had no idea what it meant to terminate a pregnancy.

We dove headfirst into having a new edition for our family. I was naïve, lacked knowledge and experience. As my mother went about preparing for this change in our lives, I realized that not only my life was changed forever, but so was my family's. Having a baby would change the lives of everyone in my immediate family. Everyone was impacted.

During this time, the relationship between my mother and stepfather was suffering, and this certainly didn't help things. How could my mother give the necessary attention to her own relationship when my premature engagement in adult activities left me in need of all of her attention. Listen carefully when I say that I was left literally carrying the responsibility of having a child, and my mother was left carrying me and my responsibility. He, the person that I engaged in the activity with, was not. His life continued as if nothing happened. His mother did not have to bear this burden. She was not inundated with doctor's appointments and the necessary tasks that come with preparing for a baby. The baby's father and his family did do their best to provide for my daughter as she grew up, but the point I am making here is that I, the female, literally carried the consequence of the choices I made.

As you know, I was kicked out of the high school, and very soon after finding out I was pregnant, I visibly wore the shame on my body. It couldn't be hidden. People stared at me all the time, making me feel small and embarrassed. As I walked along with family members, they too wore my shame. My mother was only thirty-four years old at the time and would be called granny at the young age of thirty-five. These are some of the results from the choices that I made to have sex and have a baby before I was ready. I had freedom to choose. I chose without having knowledge of what I was getting myself into. I was immature, unprepared, and motivated by my scars, but there are no excuses. When we make adult decisions, we deal with the consequences.

Tell Someone!

I had some horrible events occur to me throughout my childhood. I did not choose these incidents, nor did I have any part in the initiation of them. These incidents produced scars that I thought for decades were unhealable. I honestly thought I was unable to heal from them. Now I know different; how great is our God! This topic is exceedingly difficult. It will be difficult for some to read, as it is difficult for me to write about. In this book, I won't give details, but if you want to heal in the area of sexual abuse, I will have another book coming soon that may help you.

Victims of molestation almost always feel that they, in some way, are responsible for the assault against them. They feel violated, tainted, ashamed, and robbed. They often feel the best thing for them to do, is keep it to themselves. They wallow in self-blame and shame. This is often accompanied by the fear of some sort of retaliation or negative consequence if they tell someone. According to research, these feelings are some of the typical emotions of molestation or rape, often reported by adults. But what if the victim is a child? Or even still, what if it is a group of children. And what if the initial act started as a game, by trusted people or family? What if it happened so often, it became almost normal? What if it went on for years, even after individuals (victims) were adults? What if the normalcy of the act of sexual abuse desensitized the victim so that when different perpetrators that weren't family members tried similar acts, the victim had no voice? When do you make the choice to tell? Well, I didn't. Another victim molested alongside me told, but not for many years when the scars got in the way of adult life. The choice not to tell was an unconscious choice to live with and carry around the torment of those childhood scars for most of my adult life. The choice I made had numerous consequences, but primarily a struggle with intimacy in every relationship that I was in. The impact included dragging other people into that experience and me reliving that experience every time there was an explanation needed about sexual intimacy.

So, I have two messages here about the freedom to choose. The first one is, choose to scream your head off until you are heard! If the first person does not hear you, go to the next person. If you exhaust your resources in your immediate circle, you can always tell someone at school, or work, or church, or better yet, you can call 911. There is also a National Sexual Assault Telephone Hotline, 800.656. HOPE (4673). The damage it causes to keep it in is far worse than what may happen if you tell someone! I say this from experience. If you tell someone, you will get someone to talk to that keeps your identity confidential; you will get support from trained people in your community; you will get someone to walk alongside you through the experience. The trained professionals will not try to file a report to the police for you; they will only do it *with* you if you want them to! So, you are still in control of your healing. You set the pace. I tried to do it alone; I tried to find healing. But every time it reared its ugly head in my life, that scar became thicker and thicker.

I know you may be afraid, and you may think no one will believe you. I know it's scary to have to prove that you were sexually violated, and yes, I know that there are people who have gotten away with this violent crime time and time again. But find the courage in God and *choose* to speak out about sexual violence! I am starting to see justice when women come forward to say they've been molested or raped, and that is a comfort for me. And as an adult, I have recognized the behavior of victims and supported them in seeking help. But I carried around that trauma for years and years into my adult life before I was relieved of carrying that burden. I'm telling you if you are a victim, *choose* to tell! The consequences of not telling wreak havoc on your life. You may not understand why intimacy is so difficult for you or why relationships continue to fail. Or you may not understand your promiscuity and think that you have an illness or a sex addiction. Choosing to tell releases you from the bondage of the act and the burden of the secret. If you are carrying this burden, hear my voice and take this as knowledge to help you make the best choice for you.

In both situations, the bondage (the act) and the burden (the secret), you are haunted by what you think are your failures, when the truth is that you have to be healed of your scars. Don't carry those scars around throughout your life. They are not your failures. But if you don't release them, they eventually creep into your relationships, your morals and values, your self-identity, and your self-worth. It doesn't matter how long ago it happened, tell someone! Release yourself from this burden, free yourself from the bondage. Oftentimes, you can be helping someone else. You may be helping them to open their eyes to recognize others that may be suffering. You are making them a resource, just as you will become a resource for others, after choosing the healing and recovery route by telling someone. You become more than a resource; you become a model.

Pursue a Secondary Education?

As a former educator, I will always say pursue an education after high school! Yes! Do it! There are so many benefits from furthering your education that span well beyond the obvious one of enhancing your career options. Going to college teaches us commitment, critically thinking, learning independence, finding your mature voice, establishing positive habits, engagement with like-minded individuals, goal-setting, navigating "life," and so much more.

When I think about freedom of choice and education, I reflect on my own personal experiences and the experiences I had with my children. I also think about my experience working in an educational environment for over twenty years.

For me personally, I didn't really know about education beyond high school, simply because I chose to grow up so fast that I missed out on learning about the opportunities. I am thankful that I discovered the opportunity to go back to school for my high school diploma, and then, ultimately, I chose to seek a college education. I was so touched by my counselor's inspiration in my life that I really wanted to be there for others, especially unfortunate children. My choice to pursue an education was a good one, but it came at a price that I couldn't see in the beginning. I could only see that at the end of the road, I would accomplish two goals, the first was to be able to take care of my children, and the second was that I would be a service to others that may struggle in the education system. What I didn't see was that pursuing my education would become the most important priority in my life, and how can that be when at the time, I had two children. After receiving my associate's degree, I was obsessed with learning. I loved finding my voice and gaining the experience to use it to help others. I loved the experience of walking across the stage and collecting that degree. My first degree symbolized the commitment and hard work that I put forth to be successful; it symbolized that I was in control, that I was capable and that I could triumph over the odds that were set against me. I was a teenage mother and told I wouldn't be anything in life. But I held in my hand a document that proved otherwise.

The bachelor's degree was even more symbolic to me. I metaphorically wore that degree as an outward display of success to those who looked down on me while I was a student in the education system. The bachelor's was my ticket to teaching, to being an employee of the education system, to being on the same level as those who looked down on me when I made mistakes and became pregnant. I was now equivalent to the ones that took from me the right to participate in high school activities that I was competent to be in. I was equivalent to the ones responsible for my well-being when I was teased relentlessly as a child. I was in a place now to protect those that may be victims, like me. I felt such a sense of accomplishment when I earned that degree and became a teacher. After completing the teaching credential program and gaining a bit of experience, I enrolled directly in the master's program. This is where my freedom of choice was inaccurate. It was during this stage in life that I really needed a recipe for decision-making.

The master's degree was bittersweet. Although a good thing, it symbolized the time away from my family. It contributed to divorce. It screamed success and failure. I didn't grasp the negative impact it would have on my loved ones. I am mature enough to recognize that now. I accept the responsibility of it, and I am dealing with the consequences.

During the time of pursuing the master's, all I saw was the benefit it would bring. I was moving like a high-speed train in my career, and promotion was in my immediate grasp. The master's was the gateway to the administration world of education. In the administration world, I could reach so many more students, touch so many more families, and even become an inspiration to adults. I had awesome mentors that taught me well how to be an education administrator. I embraced more and more responsibilities and was successful at all of them. So, when the opportunity came for me to step into a leadership role, it was the obvious route for me—being promoted also meant more time committed to work. More time away from my family. I was making blind, uninformed choices. I was blinded by what success looked like, felt like, and represented for those who may have obstacles in life. I was so driven by the negative things from my past and didn't recognize the damage I was creating for my present.

Now, let me clarify. Me going to school, securing my degrees, and trying to make a better life for myself and my children is a fabulous thing! I am very proud of myself! I don't regret it at all, it was my path, and at the time, it was the best choice. But there is a better way. I'm here to tell you! I didn't have anyone to tell me, so I did what I thought was right. It was a positive thing, a good thing.

But the better way is a way that is a bit slower and planned. A way that considers the stress and negative impacts that my absence may bring on my family. A better way is to have more knowledge of the positions I was accepting and how much of my time and energy it would require. A better way was, perhaps, waiting to pursue the master's and doctorate until my children were finished with high school. Not being self-centered and securing my own education during the same time as them.

I know they may disagree with me, and I know they are immensely proud of me, but I clearly see where I could have been more present in their life, guiding them and supporting them. My heart breaks when I see where I have failed them. So, before making great decisions that impact not only you but the people around you, be sure that you have examined all ends of the spectrum, considering the positive as well as the possible negative outcomes. The best advice I can give you is to pray. Pray and ask God for guidance. Then, be still and listen with a receptive, humble, and obedient heart.

My Children

Knowing that I personally missed out on the guidance towards post-secondary education, I was laser-focused on my children graduating high school and getting an education after high school. In fact, I myself, the mother, protector, and at that time decider of all things, may have been so laser-focused that it wasn't their dreams or desires that were being pursued; it was mine. I was determined not to fail them, to ensure they were placed on the right track to what I thought would bring them success. But my laser-focused determination about their secondary education was one of my biggest failures as a parent. I was pushing them towards my dream for them, rather than the dream they may have had for themselves. I was trying to pave their path instead of just teaching them to walk in the fruit of the spirit and giving them the freedom to make their own decisions. The Bible teaches us in Proverbs 22 (NLV), "Direct your children onto the right path, and when they are older, they will not leave it."

But there I was, doing my own thing, wanting to be a successful mother, wanting to cover all the bases, and guaranteeing that I brought them successfully from birth to adulthood. I wanted to be victorious alongside them when they received their degree. I made sure they graduated from traditional high school, something I hadn't done. I made sure they participated in all the glam and glitz of being seniors, from the letterman jacket to the class ring, to the senior prom, and even walking in graduation procession in a place of honor. They both secured a grade point average of 3.0 or higher. They both got the car they wanted and were both accepted into four-year universities. I was determined! We were going to be successful in this thing! Period, no exceptions!

My Daughter

I was confident with my daughter's choice to attend a Christian university. In fact, it was in the same city that my older brother resided in at the time, so she would have support! It was an eight-hour drive from where we lived, but that was also not problematic. We had taken that drive several times to visit my older brother. It was easy! She was extremely excited. She would be eighteen just weeks after graduation, and she was ready to embrace adulthood! She would be out of mom's house and into college life. Dormitory living was the very first space of her "own." She also had her own car, set her own curfew, and planned her own days. She came and went as she pleased. She was an adult! But she was also my innocent little girl, my mini-me. Who came up with the age of eighteen as adulthood, anyway? She wasn't ready to be away from home. And I hadn't done the proper research about the city she was going to live in. I was just laser-focused on her getting to college. It didn't take long for her to feel out of place.

When I recently researched the ethnic demographics in the city where she went to college, they listed the largest five ethnic groups in the area. African American wasn't one of them. In fact, there was less than one percent of African Americans in the city when she was there. To say she was extremely uncomfortable was an understatement. She made friends easily enough, but for a very sheltered child, she felt as if she stuck out; she felt as if all eyes were on her. Unfortunately, within the first few weeks of her arrival, my brother moved back to Southern California, so she really had no one close for comfort. In addition, her heart was spoken for. Her high school sweetheart went in a completely different direction than her. There were so many things against her. She was not placed on a solid foundation for success. She was unhappy, and her biggest fear was disappointing me. That is my failure. As her life was hers to live, it is not me that she should have been afraid to fail. Her true motivation was not rooted in her own dreams but my dreams for her.

She returned home late one night, tapping at her little brother's window. She had withdrawn from the university and chose to return to our city and get a job until she decided what she wanted to do in life. I didn't even have an opportunity to transfer her back to our city college. She was eighteen years old. She had the right to choose, and having limited background knowledge, she just chose to withdraw. She traveled a bit of a rough road for a while. Dealing with the consequences of her choices. She worked unfulfilling jobs and tried to decide what road to take. She accepted the consequences for acting so hastily, but my heart was broken because I feel I hadn't properly prepared her. The beauty of freedom of choice is that when she did select the right path for her, it was so easy for her to stay on that path because it was hers alone.

She is now an entrepreneur, owning her own beauty salon, with so many clients she can hardly keep up. She loves her business, her freedom, and her life—the life she chose for herself. I am so proud of her! Every time I make my own appointment on her website, I am overflowing with joy. It took a bit more than age eighteen for her to be able to identify what she wanted to do. She needed to get out and experience life a bit. She experienced working for a boss and knew it wasn't for her. Now she has her own space, and she is her own boss.

I thank God for placing it on my heart to raise my children in His Word. I know that I only opened the door so that they would know of His existence. I provided them with the structure and the foundation for living the life of a Christian. That is so important because peer pressure and the desire to do whatever we want are so forceful. We are born into a sinful world with a sinful nature. Like Adam and Eve, we are inquisitive and easily led astray. When we are young and eager for freedom, we are vulnerable, and Satan sits ready to make his move to take us further away from our dreams. We go against what we know is right. In fact, she and her brother came to a point where they questioned religion, but God has intervened with her. He is so *good*! The seed was planted long ago, and she returned to her Heavenly Father, just as the Bible tells us our wayward children will do. Now she shares Scriptures and sermons with me!

My Son

Now, you would think that I kind of learned the ropes from my first child, but no. I actually did not. Seven years later, I followed the same path with my son.

I was adamant about him attending a four-year university. Still, in my very laser-focused mind, the university was the best choice for him, directly from a very sheltered high school experience into the pressures and responsibilities of a four-year institution. Like his sister, he also received honors graduating. In fact, he was the top African American male in his graduating class. And I was the very proud momma.

During my son's high school year, my career excelled. I was getting my master's degree at the same time. In my rush to success, I also accepted a promotion and became the principal of a middle school. Life was good! Everything was perfect! In fact, it was more than perfect. I had successfully graduated both children from high school! That, in and of itself in my family, was cause to celebrate! I was so proud of my son and so thrilled for his future! I was ready for him to go to college and do his thing! School came so easy for him; I knew he would be brilliant.

Fearing an empty nest, I started to look for opportunities in educational leadership outside of our country. He would be so consumed by the excitement of college life, even more than he was in his senior year, that he wouldn't have too much time for me anyway. I had really transformed the failing middle school that I was charged with and was even recognized in the newspaper for changing the culture and increasing the academic achievement of the students in the school. I felt ready for another challenge. So, we made an agreement, he would pack his bag for the university, and I would pack my bag and go abroad to help in education reform on the other side of the world, in the United Arab Emirates.

His first semester went well. We skyped every now and then, and everything seemed to be moving in the right direction. When I went home for the holidays that first year, there were no warning signs, so I felt a sense of affirmation. Everything was fine. Only, it wasn't. My son needed me. He was struggling, and I wasn't there. He, too, like his sister, didn't want to disappoint me. So, I didn't know of his struggles until he was in over his head. It turns out that he is most motivated when I am close to him, with a light and steady push. But I was on the other side of the world, literally. It was a sixteen-hour flight and a twelve-hour time difference. He felt as if I was out of his reach. He felt alone. Our relationship spiraled out of control. I was broken-hearted, and so was he. We were both full of pain and struggled to connect due to the spoken and unspoken words between us.

I thought I made the right choice to send my son to a university right out of college. I thought he was ready. His grades proved he was capable. He had started to distance himself from me in his senior year. But I thought that was normal for boys. He was excited about going to college, and I was excited for him. I never even considered my daughter's situation. It had disappeared from my mind so long ago. I was running on happy adrenaline, graduating the second child, and as we know from above, I was quite committed to my own studies and career when my kids were in school.

When I reflect on those days, on the outside, we all seemed confident and prepared, ready to tackle our personal worlds. Looks are deceiving. My choice to pursue my education and career alongside my kids clouded my vision, and I eventually suffered the consequences. I didn't know my babies as deeply as I thought. My perception of their reality was skewed. On the surface, we had an awesome relationship. We were so proud of each other, and we loved each other deeply. The three of us were quite close, my son, my daughter, and me. But only on the surface. I know some may disagree with me, and that's ok. But there was something in our relationships that was murky. They didn't want to disappoint me, and I wanted to be the successful mother they were so proud of. So, we didn't tell each other our deepest feelings, concerns, and fears. Our relationship was superficial, on the surface. True feelings only surfaced when my poor babies started drowning.

Parents, look below the surface! Watch for signs that say I am not *really* ready for adult life. The signs are subtle. They are almost invisible, but when I reflect back on their time in high school, the signs were there. Save yourself the pain and loss of time. Look below the surface; use a magnifying glass. Rather than just cutting the apron string, give children increased responsibility and freedom, let them go gradually. It is so hard to recover from this tragedy. It is so hard to be separated from your child, with physical distance as well as emotional distance.

We are in the process of healing those scars now. But it didn't start until I gave it all to God. I prayed that my broken heart would be healed. I prayed that my sentiments would be softened. I felt that I did the right thing! I didn't want to accept the responsibility for his failure. I got him successfully through high school and put him into college, and that was the right thing! When we consider the fact that my son graduated with high honors and that I placed him on the next path that I felt was necessary for him to be successful in life, I didn't fail. God confirmed that in me, time and time again when I would beat myself up about the strained relationship. But I did fail at making sure he was ready. I left too soon, plain and simple, and for that, I had to apologize to him, admit my wrong, and ask for his forgiveness. It was then that healing began. He, too, confessed to his failures. His lack of attention to his studies and his overwhelming fascination with the freedoms of life. He is still paying the consequences for his actions. He was completely swallowed up by the temptations of life. But he has been humbled recently by God, and he has been placed back in my care for a reset. We are resetting him on his journey in life and resetting our relationship. God is good!

I couldn't have made it through that hardship without God. I had to constantly seek His face for guidance and healing. Once I surrendered it to God, the steps for healing were revealed to me, to us.

> Therefore, confess your sins to one another [your false steps, your offenses], and pray for one another, that you may be healed and restored. The heartfelt and persistent prayer of a righteous man (believer) is able to accomplish

> much [when put into action and made effective by God—it is dynamic and can have tremendous power]
>
> **James 5:16 (AMP)**

Parents look below the surface. I know that teenagers can drive us crazy; they want to move one hundred miles per hour! They are so anxious to lead their own lives, and we can get sucked right into that excitement. Trust me when I say, dig deep and hold on to them. Eighteen years old is not the green light to adulthood, as it is often depicted to be. Move slowly; convince your children to move slowly. They have their full life ahead of them! Together, use the decision-making recipe to make choices that are beneficial for everyone.

Key Message

I hope that I have painted a picture that you indeed have the freedom to choose in life. I have shared with you three different, life-altering choices that I made, and I have also shared the consequences. I believe that during the time I made those choices, it was the right choice for me. If I had to do it all again, now with twenty years of experience, of course, I would do it differently! That's why I am here to tell you what I wish someone would have told me. The first thing I wish someone would have told me is to develop a recipe for making decisions and stick to it! With the first question in the equation being, will this decision bring glory to God? Will the decision ease you of pain or someone else of pain and suffering? If so, *don't hesitate*. Make the decision of healing. Is it an act of love, or is it self-centered? Do you have enough background knowledge on the decision that you are about to make? This includes the basics like understanding the location around you, weighing the obstacles that you may encounter along the way. Does your decision have an impact on others? Will it positively enhance your life now or in the future without negatively affecting others? Are you supporting others in making a big decision? If so, the keyword here is support. I like to think of it as a time to educate, not dominate. Will the person, at the end, feel like the decision is still theirs? Finally, can you recover if the decision does not go as you planned? What might recovery look like? Does it impact others? What damage might be done because of your actions? Have you considered what may happen if the decision doesn't go as planned? Will you be ready to face the consequences?

If I would have asked myself these questions with the three big decisions that I shared with you, I think the decisions would have gone vastly different. Having sex before marriage does not bring glory to God! Even in my youth and ignorance, if I would have continued forward after asking myself the first question in the recipe, the answer to the second question is also *not* in my favor. I had no true knowledge of sex and intimacy between a man and woman and the impact of having sex. I was clueless, which explained my surprise when the doctor told my mother I was pregnant! With such a huge decision, I should have sought counsel. But I didn't, and I made a decision that negatively impacted everyone around me. I had no clue what the consequences were. I was *not* ready.

Freedom of choice is wonderful, especially when you are young and excited to start your life as an adult. You feel so empowered. It really is exciting! Being well informed before choosing will help you pave a much smoother road for your life. Can you make it down the rocky road? Of course, you can with the help of God. But why walk a graveled path when you can walk a smooth one?

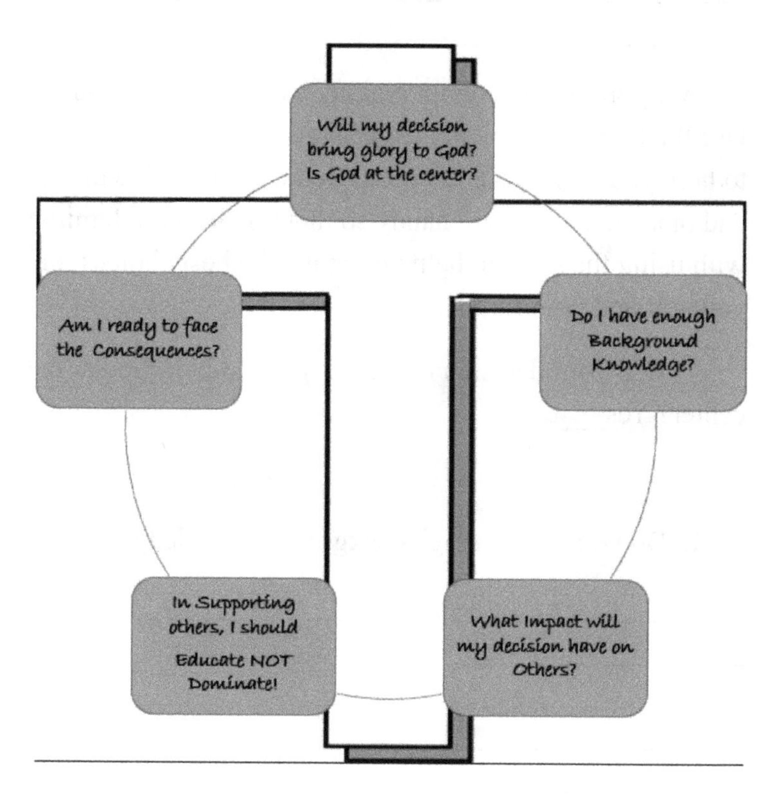

Decision Making Recipe

Think of a decision that you made in the past. If you would have followed the recipe for decision-making, would it have gone differently? Think about it and explain at which step your mind would have changed?

____

____

____

____

____

____

____

Are you thinking about making a big decision soon? Use the five questions in the decision-making recipe below to help you make your decision. Remove the recipe picture and place it somewhere handy so that you become familiar with using the steps to help you make the best choices for yourself and your family.

1. Will your decision bring glory to God? Is God at the center? Yes____ No____

2. Do you have enough background knowledge?

____

____

____

____

____

3. What impact will your decision have on others?

____

____

____

____

____

4. If you are supporting others, are you educating or dominating? If you have sought counsel in your decision, are you taking in the knowledge but still making your own decision? Or do you feel pressured to follow their advice? Remember the phrase, “Educate, don’t dominate.”

____

____

____

____

____

Have you considered the consequences? Are you ready to face them if the decision does not go as planned? What might the consequences be? Write them down to help you decide.

____

____

____

____

____

PRAYER

Heavenly Father, ruler of my life, thank You for the freedom of choice. You are not a controlling God, You are compassionate, lenient, forgiving and merciful. You let me make my own decisions, just as our ancestors Adam and Eve did. You educate me, but do not dominate me. I am the one who chooses. And even as I fail, You pick me up and teach me through the consequences of my actions. And You never leave me. You stay. Your hand reaches down to offer guidance to me again, and again and again. You are so faithful, You are so good. You are my loving father, and Your governance provides examples as to how I should parent. Lord, open my eyes so that I can see that You provide me with everything I need. I only need to seek Your counsel. You are always there, and You always will be. Thank You for Your love and steadfastness. In Jesus' name, Amen.

These are Scriptures that really speak to my spirit when it comes to freedom of choice.

They remind me that I should seek God in all choices that I make. It will take away the anxieties and give me peace and understanding. These Scriptures teach me to seek wisdom and good judgment, for ultimately, I am responsible for my decisions and must pay the consequence. Which of these Scriptures speak to you? Underline it and use it alongside the decision-making recipe to help you gain clarity.

- Make informed decisions. Gain wisdom; use the recipe.

"Get wisdom; develop good judgment. Don't forget my words or turn away from them"

Proverbs 4:5, NIV

"An intelligent heart acquires knowledge, and the ear of the wise seeks knowledge"

Proverbs 18:15, ESV

"Teach me your ways, O LORD, that I may live according to your truth! Grant me purity of heart, so that I may honor you"

Psalm 86:11, NLT

- We are made in God's image, not to fear, or worry or be anxious. Although it sounds difficult, look at this command from God to strengthen you.

"Don't be anxious about anything; rather, bring up all of your requests to God in your prayers and petitions, along with giving thanks. Then the peace of God that exceeds all understanding will keep your hearts and minds safe in Christ Jesus"

Philippians 4:6-7, CEB

The plans and reflections of the heart belong to man, But the [wise] answer of the tongue is from the LORD. All the ways of a man are clean and innocent in his own eyes [and he may see nothing wrong with his actions], But the LORD weighs and examines the motives and intents [of the heart and knows the truth]. Commit your works to the LORD [submit and trust them to Him], And your plans will succeed [if you respond to His will and guidance]

Proverbs 16:1-3 (AMP)

For each person will have to carry his own load. Let the one who is taught the word share all his good things with the teacher. Don't be deceived: God is not mocked. For whatever a person sows he will also reap, because the one who sows to his flesh will reap destruction from the flesh, but the one who sows to the Spirit will reap eternal life from the Spirit. Let us not get tired of doing good, for we will reap at the proper time if we don't give up. Therefore, as we have opportunity, let us work for the good of all, especially for those who belong to the household of faith.

Galatians 6:5-10 (CSB)

Summary

Once we become adults, we are all given the right to make our own choices. But have we been taught how to make them? Does turning eighteen come with a recipe for decision-making? No, it doesn't. It's not even something we think about. But I wish I would have had that recipe thirty-four years ago. So, now I am here to share one with you. I use it now, and I am well into adulthood, and I admit that my decisions are so much easier. They are less me-centered and more God-centered. I am of the flesh, and

I want what I want. In fact, before I started using the formula, I would rationalize with myself so that what I wanted sounded okay. But the simple fact that I had to rationalize was problematic; it should have been my red flag. Don't wait until you have made several unhealthy decisions that had adverse consequences like I did. I always did what I thought was right, and it was at the time *because* I didn't seek the counsel of my Heavenly Father. I am certain that I would have made completely different choices. Seek God's counsel in your decision-making. Freedom of choice is great, but knowledgeable, God-centered decision-making is true freedom.

Part II: I Am in Control

Oh, how I love to be in control, to be powerful and successful. How I enjoyed being looked to for problem-solving and guidance. And oh, how great it was when my plans would come together successfully. When I was successful at something, and it impacted many people, bringing positivity to those involved was one of the most rewarding feelings, a feeling that reminded me that I was in control. This was mostly at work. The professional me. The me that appeared to have it all together.

But the truth of the matter is sometimes it just looks like we are in control. Control can be an outward appearance of calm when just the opposite exists inside. Most of the time, when It seemed like I was in control, I was very much afraid inside, terrified even. But no one knew it. It was almost like I was powered by some secret forces, and because my life wasn't truly grounded, I didn't realize that I was actually powered by forces, but they are actually not so secret for those who want to know about them. All success comes from God. He equipped me with the skills needed to be successful in my work. Of course, He did! I flourished at work, and although I didn't know it at the time, it wasn't my doing. I wish someone would have told me that. I wish I would have known to be praising God for all my success in life. Then I would have also known to praise Him during my time of need. I would have known that He was there when I was in flight mode, running from the difficulties in my life. Most of my difficulties were in my personal life. This is the part of me I desperately wanted to be in control of. This is where I had to be most resilient and keep pushing forward. My personal life is where I was most haunted by my past. It is where the beginning of my character was established. My personal life is where I was determined that I was not worthy of true love. I was not in control because I was so willing to accept any love that came along, even when my gut told me it was wrong. Control would have been knowing that I was indeed truly loved; in fact, agape (pure, willful, sacrificial love) love was felt for me. God has a selfless, sacrificial, unconditional love for me that cannot be compared to that of a man. But I was so determined to get the love I was looking for that I was resilient and tried time and time again. But I was irrational, and it often left me broken and hurt.

I desperately needed a better way of making decisions because I failed miserably in my personal life. I needed a solid foundation to ground my decision in. In order to be in control, I also needed to have a more accurate sense of self. I needed to see myself in the positive light that most others saw me in, rather than allow myself to be only shaped by past experiences. Most importantly, I needed to understand God's perception of me. In having a more holistic and well-rounded view of myself, wouldn't I be more in control? If not in complete control, wouldn't I be more susceptible to start over again, well informed? Wouldn't I lose my flight character and develop a character of true perseverance, seeing myself through the obstacles, understanding that starting over again makes me stronger, bringing me closer to control.

We can all have control; of course, we can. It takes a very mystical concept called faith in God. "Now faith is confidence in what we hope for and assurance about what we do not see" Hebrews 11:1 (NIV). If we believe in God, and His Word, although we cannot see Him, we will gain control of our lives. Life becomes clear. We won't live in doubt because God's Word is the blueprint for a successful life. In His Word, we are assured that we are loved. His Word tells us that He will never leave us; and that if we are still enough, we can hear Him speaking to us in a small whisper of a voice. His Word tells us the type of person we are and gives us the tools we need to be successful in all aspects of life. Finally, His Word will show us that every time we start over again, seeking His guidance and support, the more in control we will be. Let's walk through the second half of this book together and see if we come out with a little more control over our life. I think we will.

"My salvation and my honor depend on God; he is my mighty rock, my refuge" (Psalm 62:7, NIV).

Chapter Four: How to Be Resilient and Persevere

"Consider it pure joy, my brothers and sisters, whenever you face trials of many kinds, because you know that the testing of your faith produces perseverance" (James 1:2-3, NIV).

We have just celebrated how awesome it is to have freedom of choice and how gracious and merciful our God is for loving and forgiving us in spite of the poor choices we make. I thank God for His steadfastness and for always being in my grasp to pull me out of the water, just before I drown, every single time. He is always there, just as He says He will be. Faithful.

Have you ever noticed that sometimes when we get pulled out of the water, just before we drown, we are placed on the shore, choking, heavily laden with water, and gasping for our breath; we look around for familiar faces, but there is not a person in sight. We are alone to deal with the consequences of our actions, the outcome of our choices. Dealing with consequences is okay. Dealing with them is how we grow; avoiding them is how we remain on what seems like a never-ending downward spiral. But there is an end to the downward spiral. Remember in chapter three, we talked about the *Decision-making Recipe*? We found that the most important components to the decision-making recipe were, do I have background knowledge, and am I ready to face the consequences? The recipe is the structure, but we are missing the foundation, and the foundation is the strongest part of any structure. Without a strong foundation, the structure is likely to fail.

Without structure and a strong foundation, we will keep beating ourselves up for getting in bad situations. Sometimes the situation is familiar. We have been there before. We have been pulled out of that same water time and time again. So, if the situation is repetitive, we know the consequences, right? We should have some background knowledge, right? Yet, we try and try again. What are we missing? How do we find ourselves in the same situations without growth? The answer is two-fold. The first factor is the foundation, and the most important element of all, is the still small that voice we often ignore; and the second part is the lack of deliberate self-reflection. We must purposely reflect on tough situations and learn from them. That is the only way we will grow. If we don't take the time to self-reflect after tough situations, we find ourselves in this repetitive cycle of unfortunate events.

This is crucial to understand because we will always face trials and tribulations. This is a fact of life. Whether we are Christians or unbelievers, hard times will come. Some trials we bring upon ourselves, and some we don't. But it is not the trial that is important; it is how we respond to the unfortunate experiences in life that ultimately shape our character. Typically, we find ourselves dealing with obstacles in one of the following ways. We freeze, fly, deflect, and sometimes, we are resilient and try again.

I personally am a woman of flight and resilience. I have enormous wings, and I take off when things are uncomfortable. My wings are most strong when I am hurt by someone I trust. When I am hurt, my wings are instantaneous; I don't have time to think; my wings are responding for me. Before I know it, I am soaring above the chaos, or the failure, or the fear, or the pain. I don't reflect. I am flying away to a place where I can control my environment, often a place of solitude. Alone is most familiar; I am in control, me depending on me. It is then that I gather the strength to get back on track. When I fly away from problems, I am not resilient. I do not persevere. I don't really think at all. I am operating in defense mode, protection mode. Sometimes, when it is over, I regret it, and sometimes, I don't even think about it. I am doing what I think is best for me and remember, by default, if I think it is best for me at that moment, then it is. But I will admit, when I take the time to reflect and adjust my actions, it is the only time I am resilient and persevere. Otherwise, I just keep trying and trying and trying. I am the queen of resilience. I know how to bounce back. But in some situations in my life, I missed the significance of listening and reflecting, and altering my approach before I bounce back. I didn't see the connection between listening and reflecting and then acting, eventually leading me to perseverance. This is rational resilience, and the outcome of rational resilience coupled with perseverance is what will always lead to success.

The next type of individuals are freezers. When faced

with fear, pain, or uncontrollable obstacles, they stop forward momentum all together; they freeze. Sometimes they experience decreased heart rate, restricted breathing, and a sense of dread. They can stay in bed or locked in their homes, away from people for days, literally frozen with fear. Often, they are so fearful of a situation; they never get to rectify the problem. They avoid it, at all costs. When and if they do build the courage to face the problem or reflect, the window for rectification may have passed. So they end up quite like the one who took flight, starting all over again, without the healing process of reflection. There is a positive in starting over for both the flyer and the freezer. They are learning to be resilient, not to give up. But we must be incredibly careful when we keep trying to accomplish a task that we continuously fail at without reflection. Sometimes, our resilience can be our demise. It is crucial to know when to let go and walk away and when to be resilient.

That brings us to the deflector. Those that deflect simply do not want to take responsibility for their error. They will go through great lengths to hide their mistakes or failures, or they may try to blame someone else. Deflectors cannot handle feelings of guilt, failure, or shame, so they try to justify their actions or place the blame somewhere else and deflect the attention from themselves. They rarely reflect because that means looking at themselves in the mirror and embracing their failures. Deflectors are not resilient. They do not persevere. They are typically the type of people that one day look at their lives and say, how did I end up here?

More often than not, we identify with one of these traits or, we can be a mixture of two. Or even still, certain triggers can cause us to respond in any of the three ways. Usually, we will favor only one of the mentioned responses. In fact, if you think about your responses to conflicts from your past, you may be able to identify which reaction you have. Once you identify that reaction, you will be more cognizant when it happens, and it will be easier to listen to the still small voice and depend on the *Decision-making Recipe* rather than respond in flight, freeze, or deflection.

It sounds like a difficult concept to understand, but it's much easier than it sounds.

I will share one of my stories and how I was able to learn how to let go of my flight syndrome and experience true perseverance. During my stay in the Middle East, I met a man that turned out to be a great friend. He, too, was hired to support the United Arab Emirates in their education reform. We were a small group of eleven education administrators coming in from various states in the US. We attended our trainings together and easily bonded as America was the common denominator amongst us. After our four-week training period in the capital of the Emirates, we were dispersed to the three corners of Abu Dhabi. Some of us went to Al Ain, some to the Western Region, and some remained in the capitol. I, as well as the friend I mentioned, remained in the capital. Since we had started off as a group of friends, it was only natural for us to continue to support each other. When it was time to select our housing, he and I decided to stay in the same building, and coincidently, I lived on the thirty-eighth floor and he on the thirty-seventh. We really grew dependent on each other. After long days at work, surrounded by people speaking different languages, wearing different clothing, eating foreign food, and practicing different traditions, we were mentally and physically worn out and longed for some sort of normalcy. So, we would often meet for dinner and sit and talk about our day, releasing frustrations, offering words of encouragement, or just learning from each other's experiences. Our weekly dinners became so habitual that we just made Wednesdays and Friday nights standard.

During the weekend, since we didn't have any other friends, we explored the country together. We ate at different restaurants, visited all the fancy hotels, enjoyed the beaches, festivals, and shows. We were so connected that during the weekends, when our other friends would return to the capitol for visits, they would joke about us being a couple. We looked at each other and laughed off the notion, having never considered the idea. After over a year of being close friends, the group went on a weekend getaway to a neighboring country. He and I were teased relentlessly because we sat next to each other during dinner, waited on each other while walking, and tended to engage in conversation with each other more than with the others. It was done unconsciously; we didn't even realize that it was happening; but after that trip of constant teasing, a seed was planted, and soon it became clear that we both were thinking about it. There was an elated sense of eagerness when we were planning to see each other, and we started to hug each other when we met. Most of the time, he smelled nice, but on one occasion, he had been home for quite some time and changed into comfortable clothing. When I hugged him, there was an unmistakable smell of cigarette smoke. I dismissed It, thinking maybe I got a whiff of someone's lingering odor. That was the first little voice that told me no, don't pursue a relationship with this person. This person smokes cigarettes, and you absolutely can't handle cigarette smoke. It was different when we were just hanging out because I wasn't impacted by his personal choices. However, to willingly enter into a relationship with someone who smoked? That typically would have been unheard of for me, as the smoke literally makes me sick to my stomach, but I pretended not to hear the small voice in my head. Of course, I didn't want to listen; I enjoyed receiving morning text messages that wished me a good day, now with a hugging emoji or flowers. I enjoyed it when he started to mention that I looked nice or smelled nice when we met for our weekly dinners. I enjoyed that he now made a point to open my car door or help me with my groceries to my apartment. It felt good to feel special and cared for, especially after the many failed relationships of my past. On one occasion, he decided to make me dinner. It was an early dinner, and we would take a walk along the corniche afterward to enjoy the sunset. When I entered his apartment, it was extremely dark, but it was fully light outside. The apartments had floor-to-ceiling windows, which I loved. I love the light! But it was pitch black in there. The only light was from lamps. He explained that he liked it dark; it fit his personality. I thought that comment a bit strange but ignored it. During dinner, I so longed to open the windows and enjoy the light. My inner voice was telling me, this is so not like you. What are you doing? Could you really exist in such a dark environment? But so far, his company had proven quite enjoyable, so I ignored the voice again.

A couple of weeks later, I was scheduled to have a major surgery. My best friend resided in Al Ain and would come up during the weekend, but my surgery was early in the week. I accepted his offer to help me until my best friend arrived. He was right next to me when I received my anesthesia and right there when I awoke. He cared for me during my time of recovery, and his tenderness won my heart. I started to really care for him. So, the relationship officially began. But I knew somewhere in my soul that it was not right, that we were better off friends. But I ignored my gut.

During a school holiday weekend, we decided to travel to a nearby country together. It was the first time we had gone without the whole group. It was supposed to be an intimate trip. We were becoming more serious and thought it would be good to just be alone. The trip went wrong immediately! He spilled some food on his light-colored shirt and became absolutely irate. I didn't think much of it. I thought once we arrive to our destination, just change clothes and forget about it. But he just couldn't let it go. He kept complaining about how he was a mess and how horrible it looked, and it literally ruined the entire journey to the destination. He pouted and scrubbed at the stain throughout the whole trip. By the time we arrived, I was a bit irritated. I just wanted to be alone and have some time to myself. My flight syndrome was rearing its head. I had never seen him so upset before and at something so small! I was shocked. But as I sat in my room, I became empathetic and made excuses for his behavior. That empathy came right around the time he started to flood my phone with words of apologies, embarrassment, and requests for forgiveness. Although my gut said this is definitely not a healthy way to start a relationship, I gave in, and we met the next morning, trying to pretend nothing happened. But the still small voice in my head was screaming at me, just be friends; this man isn't for you! There was obvious tension throughout the weekend, and I was happy when it was time to pack up for the return flight home. I wanted to be in the security of my own apartment. As we headed to the taxi that morning, he insisted on taking both of our bags. I was quite capable of taking my own bag and could clearly see that it would be a struggle to handle two big bags. But he insisted. I followed closely behind him, appreciating his desire to carry both bags, but having been a very independent woman my entire life, it was difficult to see him struggle with my bag! He continued to insist on handling both bags when we arrived at the airport. To avoid any further disputes, I let him. As we approached the escalator, I again offered to help; he declined. I stood back as he attempted to place the bags on the escalator. The first bag went on to the step successfully, and he stepped right on after it, but as the second bag was approaching the escalator, the decline had begun, his arms were stretched below him trying to hold the first bag, and above him struggling to stabilize the second bag on the step above him, as I reached for the bag, it was already tumbling down toward him, knocking him down. He struggled to hold the bag that was already headed down, as it would have fallen against other people. With his legs twisted and arms spread from north to south, he pressed himself against the back of the escalator for leverage and rode the entire way down in agony and embarrassment. Once he arrived at the bottom, getting up from the ground was just as chaotic. I was right behind him, but there were others behind me, and of course, we know that escalators don't slow down or stop, so it was a scramble to get him up and get moved over to the side to allow other people to pass. He shoved off my desire to make sure he was okay and grabbed the bags, and headed to the gate to board the plane. We sat in silence during the flight back to the Emirates.

My flight had kicked in, big time. I didn't want to talk about anything. I grabbed my bags from the luggage conveyer belt and found the first taxi. Once inside my apartment, I turned off my phone so I wasn't tempted to respond to his pleas for forgiveness. That night I stared up at the ceiling as I tried to fall asleep. How would I explain to him that we must remain friends? In the two years that we had been friends, we had no issues. We simply enjoyed each other's company. We were making a mistake. When I woke the next morning and turned on my phone, I was met with dozens of messages. There was also a long email of apologies and explanations of his desire to just want to care for me and please me. Throughout the day, he apologized over and over for his behavior and wanted to get together to talk. But I was in major flight mode. I was ready to throw away all the time we had together. I was ready to discard how he cared for me when I was ill, how he listened and encouraged me during hard times at work. I wanted to throw away all the good things. I was hurt, and nothing else mattered. I wanted away from him, just as I flew away from every other relationship when times got tough.

After about a week, flowers were delivered to my school, followed by text messages and invitations for dinner. Despite the still small voice warning me to remain friends, we reconciled. And, once again, the relationship was great! Perhaps, the problem was that he was trying too hard to impress me. Maybe he didn't have an anger problem. Over time, we grew more fond of each other and even started talking about marriage. I was certainly interested in marriage. I knew marriage was right in the eyes of God, and I longed to have a proper relationship with a man who would care for me and love me, one I could depend on. I had never depended on anyone for fear of abandonment, but now that I had someone to care for me, I loved the comfort it brought. If we really wanted to be together, in the country we were living in, we had to be married; it was the law. Plus, things were going great. There were no real incidents outside of road rage, but everyone drove crazy in the Middle East, so that didn't bother me too much.

We started to plan the wedding. We looked for rings, decided on the location, and shared plans with family. Although apprehensive, my family was happy. They can clearly see he spoiled me and cared for me, and they were happy that I finally had someone to lean on. His family was not as accepting, as he and I did not share the same nationality. He didn't seem to care much about their opinions; he said the relationship was already very strained and barely existent, so we didn't pay much attention to their disapproval. I didn't think much about their strained relationship, although it was a huge red flag, and I should have. I was too busy enjoying being showered with his undivided attention and him lavishing me with any desire of my heart and other pleasant surprises that I didn't desire. For a girl that spent her life taking care of others, I couldn't help but be overjoyed by the love and care I was receiving. Months had gone by without even a hiccup, and I was really starting to look forward to our union the following summer. We decided to take another trip for New Year's. He wanted to take me to Italy. I was so excited. He planned a beautiful ten-day trip, where we would spend a few days in Florence, followed by Christmas in Venice and New Years' in Rome. We were so excited. We packed lots of clothing to suit every occasion; four suitcases total.

Our time in Florence was amazing. It was so beautiful with so much to see, great food to eat, and an awesome culture to experience. Everything was going fabulous; I was even allowed to help with the luggage, which was important since we ultimately had three destinations during the trip. When arrived in Venice, the second leg of our trip, I was quite exhausted, and I needed rest, but we clearly were not aligned with our intentions for the evening. Before I knew it, we were having a disagreement. In just seconds, the conversation escalated; he walked out of the room, slamming the door behind him. Worn-out, I laid on the bed, thinking this will all be over in the morning. But I was wrong. He returned to the room, repacked his bag, and announced that he was leaving. I sat there in disbelief. I pleaded with him to just rest tonight, and we can discuss it in the morning. But he wasn't having it. He literally packed his bags and left me sitting in a hotel room in Venice, Italy.

Now that you have a picture of the cycle of our relationship, months of bliss, followed by his fits of rage, me flying and not discussing the problem, followed by my gullible forgiveness. On and on it went. Now, one may argue that I was resilient, even in my flight. Resilience is to recover from difficult situations. I believe I had resilience mastered. In fact, it was mastered so well that this was not my first unhealthy relationship. I had been in plenty before. All ending without the conversation and healing required for growth. Without my personal reflection on my contributions to the failure. I would simply remain in and out of the crazy cycle of negativity until I just couldn't take it anymore. Then my wings would take me far away from the predicament, so far that I would close the door on that chapter and add another layer of scar to already scarred *heart* tissue.

The Italy scenario was not the end of that chapter, after several weeks of alone time and messages of apologies and love. I forgave him again. But we never reflected on the situation, and we didn't seek help for his fits of rage. He did disclose incidents of childhood trauma that were certainly the root of his anger. He only promised to be better, and I believed him. He was so convincing, and honestly, I truly believed he was sorry every time. I was engaging in unhealthy resilience. I was not reflecting and seeking help. I wasn't paying attention to the still small voice. So, we did marry. But we never had the chance to live together as husband and wife. Shortly after the wedding, as we looked for our new home together, he had another episode. This one was a bit different. He was ranting and raging and was quite in my face. He was upset with the fact that we were married but still lived separately, him in the apartment below mine. I understood his feelings, but something in me felt better with him in the downstairs apartment. It had been working for us for so long that it felt right for me. I believe I was honestly afraid not to have my own space to flee to, so I didn't pursue having a space together with the same sense of urgency as he did. So, he was very frustrated with me.

He had never invaded my space before, and I was immediately taken back to previous relationships of domestic violence. I remembered jumping from the balcony of an upstairs apartment; I remembered a broken jaw and stitches in my arm; I remembered being afraid. I put as much space as I could between myself and him and tried to reason with him. Again, he wasn't having it. He took off his wedding ring and threw it at me, hitting my right cheekbone just underneath my eye. As I screamed, he instantly regretted his actions and tried to console me. But I knew right then that I was finished giving him chances. My resiliency was gone. At that moment, I knew that I needed to end this chapter. I knew that if I remained in that relationship with him, that it was only going to get worse. Now, he showed me he was physically abusive, and I would not do that again. That relationship, like others I was in, never received the outside support it needed in order to persevere. My constant flight, and excusal of the problem, ensured the situation was doomed. I was broken-hearted. My spirit was broken, and I was alone. I was determined that I was completely over relationships and trusting men with my heart. I always seemed to attract the same type of men. Relationships had proven to be nothing but failure for me, time and time again. Now here I was thousands of miles away from family. My best friend had returned to the States to live, and I found myself utterly alone.

As I reflected on this incident and previous relationships, I can clearly see the root causes of my bad decision-making. The most vital cause is ignoring the small voice that warned me not to enter into a bad situation. I am using relationships as my example because all of my intimate relationships were epic failures, regardless of the fact that I was resilient. I kept forgiving; I kept trying. But my resilience was unhealthy resilient. I lacked discernment. My judgment was skewed. I continued to ignore the voice, although it warned me time again about the same topic. To say I was hardheaded is putting it lightly. The good thing is that the voice is steadfast, always there, warning me again and again about the same old topics, as well as new topics. The voice was always with me. When I don't take heed to the voice and practice self-reflection, I am not practicing healthy resilience; I am perpetuating an unhealthy cycle. In this way, I would never persevere in the area of relationships.

The other root cause of my failed relationships was me looking for love in the wrong places. You know what happens when you keep looking for something in the wrong place? Yep, you will continue to find the wrong thing! And as you can see, I have had my share of bad relationships. Each time I committed myself to the relationship, I distinctly remember the still small voice telling me not to engage. Not only was the voice telling me not to engage, but it was also showing me clearly, that I should not engage—every single time. But I wanted my way. I wanted whatever immediate satisfaction that relationship was going to give me. Most often, it was love. Or what I thought was love. I wanted unconditional love, and I was willing to be resilient to get it. I wanted to persevere in the area of relationships in my life. I wanted success. I thought for sure that each new relationship was the right one. I had been praying for years for a successful relationship, and I was sure God would bless me. However, after the relationship I just shared with you, I was finished. I was only interested in friendship. Because I was broken, I turned to God for comfort. And he was there. He had always been there, warning me. God is that still small voice. He is the strong foundation of the *Decision-making Recipe.*

I am using relationships as an example because it has been my recurring obstacle in life, but it doesn't matter what the situation is. If you have found yourself trying the same thing over and over again but only experiencing failure, you most certainly understand resilience, but what's missing? Are you practicing rational resilience? In order to persevere, your resilience has to be rational. That means every time you fail or experience an obstacle, you have to reflect, and you have to seek God's guidance. Perseverance is the continued effort to do or achieve something despite difficulties, failure, or opposition, despite the delay in achieving success. But you will never experience success if your resilience isn't rational. If you are chasing something you shouldn't be, or if you haven't paid attention to the still small voice warning you not to engage, you will continue to fail. Once you have tried and tried to be successful at something and are no closer to success than you were the first time, you may feel like I felt. "*I give up*!"

I personally gave up on having a successful relationship, even though I knew in my heart that I was made for marriage. I was made to be in a family. I wanted to love and be loved. But I was tired of the failure. Have you reached your end? If so, let me tell you something I wish someone would have told me. *Listen to the still small voice.* It is not just the pessimistic side of you trying to deter you from your goal. It is so much bigger than that. It's bigger than anything you can ever imagine. When that voice is trying to guide you away from something you know you shouldn't do, it is God. When you know deep in your gut that you shouldn't engage in a situation, and you are affirmed by the still small voice, then don't do it. I could have saved myself so much heartache if I had only listened to the Holy Spirit inside me. But let's go beyond my story; let's look at the best book there is to guide us.

Have you heard of the story of Elijah in the book of 1 Kings? Elijah was a prophet of God. He was obedient to God but had many trials along his journey of life. But Elijah was resilient and continued to follow God's Word. In fact, he was rationally resilient because, as a prophet, he communicated with God. He was eventually triumphant in proving that the Lord was the one true God, whereas King Ahab and Jezebel worshiped Baal, and the people of Israel, went back and forth between the two. But God won't have this. The people were to either follow God or follow Baal. Elijah held a competition between Baal and the Lord. Both needed to light the prepared alter using fire, which was supposed to Baal's strength. The one who would light the alter using fire was the one true god. The prophets of Baal called upon him for hours, asking him to bring down fire to light the altar; they called on him so long that Elijah mocked them, telling them to call louder, call louder! But when Elijah called upon God, His fire came down from heaven and consumed everything in and around the alter. Baal was defeated in the eyes of the people. Elijah's rational resilience led the Israelites to believe that God is the one and only true God. The people of Israel bowed down to God, and the prophets of Baal were slaughtered.

But the results did not go as Elijah expected. Jezebel, in her wickedness, still would not believe. Even though Elijah continued to show resilience and determination, praying to God for rain to end the three-year drought, she ordered his death. Out of fear, he ran away into the woods to escape the wrath of Jezebel. He was discouraged and wanted to die, yet he continued to be resilient with a continuous prayer to God. He arrived at Mt. Sinai. Where God communicated to him to stand on the mountain before the Lord as he passed by, here he experienced a strong wind, then a huge earthquake, and a raging fire. But God was in none of those huge intense elements. Suddenly, Elijah heard a small still voice, and Elijah knew it was God. When he listened, God spoke to him and asked him what he was doing in the cave? When Elijah was still and heard God's instruction, it was revealed to him what he needed to know. His strength and faith were restored, and he was given the wisdom to move forward. The Scripture reads,

> Then He said, "Go out, and stand on the mountain before the LORD." And behold, the LORD passed by, and a great and strong wind tore into the mountains and broke the rocks in pieces before the LORD, but the LORD was not in the wind; and after the wind an earthquake, but the LO RD was not in the earthquake; and after the earthquake a fire, but the LORD was not in the fire; and after the fire [a]a still small voice. So it

> was, when Elijah heard it, that he wrapped his face in his mantle and went out and stood in the entrance of the cave. Suddenly a voice came to him, and said, "What are you doing here, Elijah?
>
> **1 Kings 19:11-13 (NKJV)**

Does any of this sound familiar to you? Have you heard the still small voice of God asking you what you are doing here, making you reflect on your choices? And when you were still enough to listen, doesn't he give you the instructions to persevere? He showed Elijah that he didn't have to run. He gave him instructions on how to try again and be successful. He also gave me instructions when I was still enough to hear Him. He said, stop seeking love; God revealed to me that the only love I needed was His love and that I didn't need to seek the love of a man. As He comforted me, He showed me that He would care for me and He would love me. So, I started to spend my time with Him for healing and guidance. I needed to let go of my fears and desires and listen closely to that small voice giving me the wisdom to be successful with the affairs of my heart. I wasn't even showing God that I could love myself. I ignored His warnings and continued to place myself in unhealthy situations. I am not only speaking of this relationship, but I am also speaking of all the ones before it as well. I was leaning on my own understanding rather than listening to the voice that kept trying to teach me the right way.

First and foremost, I needed to strengthen my relationship with God. I needed to call on Him daily, not just during the waves of highs and lows. I was notorious for praising Him when things were fabulous and calling on Him when things got hectic. I needed to seek His face daily! That is where my energy should be. How could I love the man God was preparing for me, If I didn't first love God and myself? I had been praying for a man of God for so many years, but I never waited on the Lord to answer my prayers. I took matters into my own hands, ignoring God's guidance. But He heard my cries for a Godly man. He heard them long ago, and He is always faithful in His timing, blessing us when we are ready to receive His blessings. As I waited, I needed to work on myself and listen for guidance. A message I heard loud and clear, and one that I hope you also hear, is if you desire an intimate relationship, one of the first conversations should be ensuring that both people desire a relationship with God and desire Him to be the center of their union. Without God, our judgment is erratic.

I needed better judgment; I needed discernment. I needed to know when God was talking to me. It is the key ingredient to being resilient and persevering. Discernment leads to rational resilience so that you can ultimately persevere and experience success. Discernment knows when to let go. The Bible tells us that "I, wisdom live together with good judgement. I know where to discover knowledge and discernment" (Proverbs 8:12, NLT). That small voice is trying to give you wisdom and discernment. God wants only the best for us. He is steadfast, constantly talking to us, trying to guide us. But remember, He also gives us choice. The Bible goes on to reveal that, People without discernment are doomed (Hosea 4:14, CSB).

Hear me clearly, if you keep failing at something, no matter how hard you try, I encourage you to stop and pay attention to the still small voice. Your resilience in that area of failure can ultimately be your demise because that resilience is flat out disobeying your Father, and although our Heavenly Father is forgiving, He will also use your stubborn resilience as an opportunity to open your eyes, just as He did for the people of Israel time and time again.

People of Israel

The people of Israel were God's chosen people. In the Book of Exodus, God used Moses to lead them out of the brutal slavery and bondage of Egypt, and initially, they were thankful. They were rescued from inhumane treatment, from harsh labor, from beatings, and from the killings of their sons. The Pharoah of Egypt was monstrous; he was the worst character in the Bible at the time. And the people of Israel rejoiced when God defeated the Pharaoh by swallowing up him and his army in the Red Sea. After that victory, the people sang to the Lord, the first song of worship recorded in the Bible. But once hardship came, the people started to doubt. They constantly complained and even asked Moses why they were rescued from Egypt just to die in the desert. They didn't remember the hard times of Egypt; they could only remember that they ate fish and drank water daily. Although the Israelites complained constantly, God blessed them with water. In fact, even though they appeared ungrateful, God entered into a covenant with the Israelites. They were to follow His laws and become priests to spread the Word of God across the nations, and

He was to be their God. Without hesitation, the people all agreed. But when Moses was up on the mountain working with Lord to construct the laws, the people started to complain again. They felt Moses was taking too long. Before Moses could return from the mountain, the people had already broken the two first laws of the Lord and built an idol of a golden calf to worship. God was brokenhearted and angered. So quickly, the people forgot about their promises to follow the laws of God. But God forgave them, and they tried again; they appeared ungrateful and continued to fail. They were not reflective people, considering their errors. They quickly forgot about their sins against the Lord and took his forgiveness every time, and tried to follow again without correction. They didn't freeze in their tracks when obstacles came their way. They also didn't fly away. They were resilient and followed God after they received whatever they were complaining about, often food or water. They were deflectors. Never truly taking responsibility for their actions, blaming their predicaments on each other. After constant moaning and complaining about hunger, God blessed the people with bread from heaven. They would wake up to it every morning; they called it manna. Soon, the people began complaining again. Now they wanted meat! They were not grateful for the manna, and it wasn't just plain bread; it is explained to be like coriander seed and tasted like wafers made with honey. But they complained.

Now, remember I spoke about looking for things in the wrong places. Well, similarly, the Israelites were complaining about things constantly. They complained as much as I looked for love in the wrong places, and guess what? They eventually got exactly what they complained they were lacking. In the book of Numbers 11:18-21, Moses shared with them that will eat meat! In fact, they will eat it until it came out of their ears until they were sick of it. For thirty days, they would eat meat. The Scripture reads,

> Now tell the people, "Purify yourselves for tomorrow; you will have meat to eat. The LORD has heard you whining and saying that you wished you had some meat and that you were better off in Egypt. Now the LORD will give you meat, and you will have to eat it. You will have to eat it not just for one or two days, or five, or ten, or even twenty days, but for a whole month, until it comes out of your ears until you are sick of it. This will happen because you have rejected the LORD who is here among you and have complained to him that you should never have left Egypt."

Numbers 11:18-21 (GNB)

Let's not be like the people of Israel. Let us be resilient in our hard times, listening to God, reflecting on our situation, being thankful for His grace, and moving towards perseverance. When we complain about our situation or chase after the wrong thing, over and over again, regardless of the voice of God warning us to be still and listen to His instructions, we will ultimately get what we are looking for. Remember, our resilience can be our demise, as it was with the people of Israel. They constantly complained and were so ungrateful and sinful that they themselves never saw the promised land. They died in the wilderness while their children inherit the promised land. Don't you want to experience perseverance to succeed? I do! That's why I am here to tell you what I wish someone would have told me. Listen to the still small voice. Reflect on your actions and make corrections before moving forward. Seek God's guidance; He is always with us. He will never leave nor forsake us.

The Still Small Voice—Life Changing

A final story has been placed on my heart to share with you. It is the story about me becoming a Christian author. As you know, I was an educator for over twenty years. I absolutely loved my job, and I was great at it. I felt like I was born to be an educator. But slowly and surely, it just wasn't resonating with my soul any longer. My job became tedious and unnatural. I thought it was the new position I had taken when I returned to the US. So, I was resilient and just kept at it. But I was starting to sound like the Israelites! I was constantly complaining. After lots of conversation and prayer, my husband and I decided that I would quit my work in education and just be still and wait for God to point me in the direction I should go. I desperately wanted to know what I should be doing with my life. I have always served people in education so, I thought for sure that I would step into a new position in education, one that was more challenging and less restrictive. I started looking at recruiting websites and filling out applications for district office positions. I had several interviews and put in ten times more applications than I had interviews, only to be rejected. It seemed that this wasn't the path that I was supposed to take. But I tried, over and over again. I even flew to other states to interview and was offered a position that I just couldn't take. It was unrealistic to work in one state while my life was in another. I was trying so hard that I wasn't being still at all! I spent hours every day on my computer looking for jobs or contemplating starting my own business, utilizing my Doctorate in Social Justice. It seemed like the perfect solution because it was right around the time when our country was experiencing quite a bit of racial tension with the constant police brutality and murders of people of color. But the business ideas and applications for leadership in social justice never came to fruition.

It came to me one day that I should start writing again. I could finally expand on my article on *Balanced Teaching* and finally write the book. I had started a book on education many times before but just couldn't gain momentum. But I was resilient. One day I sat at my computer with my head down, waiting for the ideas to flow, and I heard a still small voice telling me to share my life experiences with others. The voice told me that people could learn from my life experiences and that I should start a book called *Messages to Those Who Come After Me*. What!? I almost went into freeze mode because God had removed fleeing from my options. I was already without work, and the world was plagued by the COVID-19. Where would I go? This couldn't possibly be what I was supposed to be doing with my life. This can't be my calling. I am a teacher! I sat frozen, and the still small voice whispered, people will certainly learn from my messages, so stop procrastinating and start writing. When I listened to the voice and started writing, I found it easy to get the words on paper. In fact, it was therapeutic. All of a sudden, I started seeing God's blessings in my life. Often, I am brought to tears, and other times I am giddy with excitement because I could clearly see how others could learn from my experiences.

When I got to Chapter Two, I submitted my partial manuscript to Christian publishers and was offered a writing contract. How do I even put my joy into words! I can't. All I can say is that I experience such a state of peace when I am writing about how good God has been to me. I am so thankful that God is persistent yet patient. I am so glad that I took the time to listen to Him. I was hardheaded; as you can see from my experiences, I can be. I thought for sure I should be looking for a job in education, teaching children or administrators, but I was wrong. I am supposed to teach people about the glory of God through my messages.

What about you? What type of person are you when it comes to dealing with life's conflict or obstacles?

Do you freeze, fly, or deflect? Are you resilient and persevere? How do you respond to fear? Take a moment to think about tough times from your past, consider at least three to four. What was your immediate response? Do you see a pattern? Write down what type of person you are in times of conflict or obstacles. ______________________

____

____

Think about a time when your desires were more important to you than the still small voice. What were those desires? ______________________________

____

____

What was the still small voice instructing you to do?

____

____

____

Did you reflect after the incident? If so, what did you learn? ________________________________

____

Were you rationally resilient? Did you move forward to experience perseverance in that area of your life? ________

____

____

____

Finally, what can you do to spend less time in freeze, flight or deflection mode? What words can you use to catapult yourself out of those negative responses to obstacles in life. ____________________________________

____

____

I have started to look at the Decision-making Recipe. I ask myself, do I have enough background knowledge about the situation I am going to engage in? Will my actions glorify God? Can I deal with the consequences if I fail? And have I listened to the still small voice trying to guide me? If I can answer yes to all of these questions, I can confidently move forward with the decision. I will celebrate my successes and learn from my mistakes. Ultimately, I will be building my character and, hopefully, deepening my relationship with my Lord and Savior.

PRAYER

Oh, Heavenly Father, colossal in power, massive in stature, omniscient, and omnipresent, but with a still small voice. I praise Your Holy Name! Lord, we couldn't handle it if You were to speak to us in Your glorious and mighty full voice! We can barely handle Your whisper. Lord, You know Your stubborn children. You know that even though You are constantly whispering to us, we will yield to the flesh time and time again. Thank You, Father, for not giving up on us. Lord, some of us freeze, some of us fly and some of us deflect when times get tough, but I thank You, God, for showing us how to be resilient. Thank You for giving us multiple opportunities to try and fail. Lord, it builds our character, it makes us reflect on who we are, and who we should strive to be. Lord, I understand that our trials are inevitable and necessary and pushes us to stay grounded in Your Word; this makes us rationally resilient. Lord, it is only through You that we can experience true perseverance in our difficult obstacles. Lord, thank You for revealing the Decision-Making Process with You as the foundation to help us make solid decisions. Lord, without You we run in circles, chasing the wrong thing. The sooner we put You as the center of our life, those circles we run will stop. With You at the center, we are most aligned with the Holy Spirit, who makes our path straighter. Lord, I thank You for always being with me, and I especially thank You for Your still small voice, giving me affirmation of Your presence, building my faith. Lord, I love You. In Jesus's name, I pray. Amen.

A Word About Spousal Abuse

Spousal abuse is unacceptable. Whether it is verbal, physical, abandonment, or psychological abuse. It is flat-out wrong, should not be tolerated, and is not accepted by God. For all of those who have suffered spousal abuse, I want to say I understand why you stay. You love your spouse; you truly believe the person is capable of change. In my personal experience, there were two things missing from every abusive relationship I allowed myself to be in. The most important thing was my personal relationship with God, and the second was his relationship with God. Without those two things, abuse relationships will never be successful. If we have a relationship with God, we strive to be like Him, and we know He is gentle and kind. He is full of kind words and love. He tells us we are His, we are forgiven. He first loved us, so we know how to love others. If you or your spouse don't have a relationship with God. I hope the Holy Spirit reaches you through my message. Seek God. Seek help from your church. God forgives abusers if they repent with their whole heart, and God heals the abused. Father, help us with this struggle. Show us how to abide in your love. In Jesus' name, Amen.

These are Scriptures that really speak to my spirit when it comes to being resilient and persevering. I have also included Scriptures on God's communication to us. These

Scriptures remind me that wisdom and guidance come from the Lord. They remind me not to lean on my own understanding but to trust in Him in all that I do. It is only then that I can be resilient during hard times and persevere.

- When you feel led to keep company that you know you should not consider this verse.

  Let no one deceive you with empty words, for because of these things the wrath of God comes upon the sons of disobedience. Therefore, do not become partners with them; for at one time, you were darkness, but now you are light in the LORD. Walk as children of light (for the fruit of light is found in all that is good and right and true) and try to discern what is pleasing to the LORD.

  Ephesians 5:6-10 (ESV)

- When you feel compelled to follow your own ways, ways of the flesh, consider this Scripture.

  "Do not be conformed to this world, but be transformed by the renewal of your mind, that by testing you may discern what is the will of God, what is good and acceptable and perfect"

  Romans 12:2 (NRSV)

- When you need to hear the Word of God, consider this Scripture.

  "And after the earthquake a fire, but the LORD was not in the fire; and after the fire a still small voice".

  1 Kings 19:12 (KJV)

- Because God shows us mercy, love, and grace, we should strive to be Christlike. Read this Scripture for motivation.

> For this very reason do your best to add goodness to your faith; to your goodness add knowledge; to your knowledge add self-control; to your self-control add endurance; to your endurance add Godliness; to your Godliness add Christian affection; and to your Christian affection add love.

2 Peter 1:6 (GNT)

- When we need to work on our character through trials and tribulations, read this Scripture.

> "We can rejoice, too, when we run into problems and trials, for we know that they help us develop endurance. And endurance develops strength of character, and character strengthens our confident hope of salvation".

Romans 5:3-4 (NLT)

- When you are discouraged, read this Scripture for motivation.

> "For I can do everything through Christ, who gives me strength".

Philippians 4:13 (NLT)

Key Message

We all have a response to conflict, pain, and obstacles.

Some of us freeze, some of us fly, some of us deflect, and some are resilient and persevere. It is important for me to mention this because if you find yourself stuck in one of these patterns and not moving forward in your life, I want to tell you, you are not alone! I have a message for you! We don't have to be constrained by these emotions and responses. It may seem like there is no way out, but I am proof that there is. You can be rationally resilient and persevere, ultimately experiencing success in all the difficult situations of your life.

I have always been a child of flight, especially as it pertains to relationships. I was very resilient but had never persevered and been successful in an intimate relationship. When things were uncomfortable, I flew. I never took the time to reflect, heal, and modify my approach. Sure, I started a different relationship; but all relationships have their challenges, which means I would fly again. And although I prayed for success in a relationship, I ignored it when God was trying to guide me.

If you want to end your negative response to conflict, pain or obstacles, and experience perseverance in those areas, the single most important thing to do is listen to God. He is always talking to us, always trying to guide us. Listen and respond; use the Decision-making Recipe and end the repetitive cycle of unfortunate events. I promise it will work. God has blessed me, and I am married again to a man that loves the Lord; and like previous relationships, this one has its challenges. They all will! But I listen to God, and I seek His guidance. When I feel like flying, I fly to Him for comfort, understanding, wisdom, and the strength to be rationally resilient. In this relationship, I will persevere; I will be successful because God is the foundation. You, too, can end your flight, freeze, or deflecting. Just give it a try, listen to the still small voice, and persevere. The feeling of success will boost your spirit, strengthen your faith, and build your character.

Chapter Five: I Am a Leader

"For by the grace given to me I say to everyone among you not to think of himself more highly than he ought to think, but to think with sober judgment, each according to the measure of faith that God has assigned" (Romans 12:3, ESV).

If someone were to ask you to describe yourself in three sentences or less, what would you say? What if they provided you with this sentence frame? I am ________. I enjoy_______. I aspire to ______. Can you immediately fill in the blanks? I would like to engage in an activity with you. The activity is called "Who am I?" At the end of the activity, you will be able to describe yourself in three sentences to anyone who asks. If you don't currently like who you are, you will be able to add a spin to the sentence to depict that you are a work in progress, which most of us are. Our activity has four parts. The first part is to self-reflect on how you came to be who you are today, right now, at this moment in time. You may start by thinking about experiences in life, in your childhood during adolescence, during your education, or your work experiences. I will indulge you by reflecting and sharing some of my personal experiences and how I came to be who I am today. The second activity I want us to do is to look at a list of character traits and find fifteen that describe you. The third part is to reflect on how others may characterize you or influence how you characterize yourself. Finally, we will look into a mirror and articulate what we see or what we want to see. Our final activity, at the end of the chapter, will be to take all four activities and write a letter to ourselves describing who we are now and how we came to be. We can also express to ourselves who we aspire to be in five years, and finally, summarize who we are in a few sentences, no more than three. I will then assist you in writing out your five-year goal, including milestones to measure our progress along the way. Don't worry; I will do all of this myself and provide you with a model to go by. Just promise me you will engage in this activity, and I will promise you that you will have a clearer picture of who you are and who you want to be. I will start with activity one, my reflection, to encourage you in your self-reflection. I hope you enjoy this chapter!

Activity Part I—*My Self-Reflection: How I Became Me?*

One day, I awoke and found myself the matriarch of my family. They all looked to me for guidance and decisions. I was the one gathering the family together for celebrations, and I was the one leading tough decisions as well. Somewhere in my adult life, I transitioned from the girl that would add to the statistics of teenage pregnancy and African Americans on welfare to the rock of my family. It happened so gradually that I didn't even see it happening. The first event that I remember taking control of is my grandfather's funeral in 2007. My mom, uncles, and aunts just couldn't agree on anything. Sadly, in 2006, just one year earlier, we buried my grandmother. But no one had to do anything; she had it all planned out for us, including the flowers! Because of the inability to agree and the distraction of other family concerns, myself and my two older female cousins took the reins and started to plan the service. We wrote the eulogy, collected pictures for the programs, and supported the funeral conductors in how we wanted the services to go. I believe our parents appreciated the fact that we took over, and it came so naturally to all three of us.

After that event, it seemed my immediate family looked to me to make family decisions. I was newly married and was working really hard at my education and career. I suppose I appeared to be quite stable. I was dedicated to grow, and I was definitely moving forward in life. I made certain that my family went to church regularly, went to work and school daily, we celebrated holidays and birthdays, and planned family getaways. The kids were given responsibilities to build their capacity, and life was routine. Most family events happened at my house. I enjoyed being looked upon for guidance, support, and encouragement. I embraced it. It felt natural. Leadership felt natural. Was it because I felt so invisible and shunned as a child that I enjoyed being seen and recognized as being a person of value? I'm not really sure; I just knew that anything I took charge of turned out successful. It turned out good. Even when I wasn't sure it was going to.

I remember an experience as a high school Activities Director, where I got myself in a situation that should have turned out disastrous. I was fairly new in the position, and I was really enjoying the experience. One of the responsibilities was to organize the school pep rallies. These pep rallies were held in the school gym and would typically be held on Fridays before big athletic games. The school had over 3000 students, so it was necessary to split the students into three groups so that all students enjoyed the experience. During the first pep rally of the day, my team of ASB students (associated student body or student government), whom I taught every day, prepared the gym for the event. They were experienced in running the events alongside me, as all events were voted on by them, organized by them, and planned in class by them, with my guidance, before we conducted the events. During the events, they created class competitions using all sorts of silly games, the school band performed as well as the cheerleaders and other school clubs. For the most part, I was the one responsible for the entire event, as my team was a group of students, children. Typically, the event begins with teachers escorting their classes into the gym and sitting in their assigned areas. This happens fast, as the kids and the adults want to get to the fun activities and competitions. They want to celebrate the players, and watch the performances, and get, well, pepped up; it is a pep rally! On this particular day, the competition called for several students from each grade level to come down to the gym floor to participate in the game. Ten students from each grade level brought forty students to the floor. My team of ASB students was twenty-five, and the cheerleaders were about forty-five students. So, on the floor at the time were over 100 students. This was acceptable; it was normal, controllable. The four teams had to select one student to wrap like a mummy, place a top hat on its head, which contained a large beachball in the center. The student was then to walk through a flat obstacle on the gym floor and grab the winning flag. It was a super close competition with the seniors and sophomores reaching for the flag at approximately the same time but toppling over as they were mummies and couldn't rip their dressing during the race, lest they be disqualified, in the excitement and determination to prove their victory students from the senior class and sophomore class started running from the seats in the stands onto the gym floor. Music was blaring; students were cheering and screaming in excitement, and things were looking a bit scary for me. As I sat thinking of a solution, nearly all the students were out of the stands and onto the gym floor. It was literally hundreds of excited teenagers jumping around to music and laughing and having a fabulous time. As the sophomores and seniors struggled to determine who the winners were, I could see how things could easily get out of control. But they were hundreds, and I was one. Although I appeared calm and in control, I was scared and not in control at all! This was all my responsibility, and anything that happened would be my fault. Some teachers remained in the stand where their classes once sat, while others had fun on the gym floor with the students. The commotion brought the other administrators to the gym as well as the team of security guards. They all looked in my direction for instructions, as it was my event. I grabbed the microphone, turned off the music, and said, "Okay, I will announce the winner once everyone is back in their seat, *and* the grade level that is seated the fastest may just help to break the tie." All of a sudden, students were scurrying back to their seats. The security team and administrators, seeing my strategy, helped to usher students back to their seats, and in less than three minutes, the floor that was flooded with close to a thousand students was empty, and I stood in the middle with my team and my cheerleaders. I was literally shaking with a mixture of anxiety and happiness. Later that day, at the admin meeting, I was congratulated on how I handled the situation so well. I accepted the accolades and hoped my face didn't reveal the actual trauma that I had experienced that afternoon. I thanked my colleagues for responding immediately to support me, and we all chalked it up as just another day of work in a large suburban high school.

That event could have gone horribly wrong, but my team saw my strength instead of my fear. There were reassured of my abilities as a leader and continued to encourage me to move forward in my career. As a result, I was reassured of my abilities and embraced more challenges with confidence. My career progressed in depth and responsibility, and I was faced with numerous situations that tested my abilities and built my character. Soon I would test these qualities that others saw in me in another region of the world, really assessing what I perceived as my personal qualities and strengths.

I moved to the Middle East, where I would support the government in its education reform project. I was excited and ready to make a difference. During the interview process, the one question that was asked to me several times was how I would handle *leading upward*. What exactly did that mean? I was unsure but answered continuously that leadership is about understanding a goal and moving your team toward that goal. You lead by example. You jump in and demonstrate expectations, not just dictate orders. Ultimate you could lead people and not even know it as long as you have strong social skills, so leading upward wouldn't be a problem. It didn't take long to understand the concept of leading upward. I was charged with the responsibility of leading a school that was already led by a principal. I was to train the leadership team without them knowing that I was training them. But first, I had to figure out how to pass the language barrier, and that was, of course, after understanding the culture that differed drastically from mine. I had to do this while being looked at closely through a magnifying glass. Every mistake was being identified; everything that looked like incompetence to them was being recorded; I was there to help and support in a place where I wasn't initially wanted. After just a little bit of research and observation, I understood exactly where the resistance was ingrained. I arrived in year four of a ten-year education reform project. Hundreds of what they would consider foreign educators had arrived before me. This place where I dedicated my time, energy, and heart was an Arabic country. They spoke Arabic, and their faith is Islam. They had been inundated with what they considered "Westerners," telling them how to run their education system that had been established by their ancestors and their heritage. All of sudden, routines and practices that had been depended on for years and years were deemed ineffective or antiquated. Now they were swarmed with westernized ways of operating, with the accompanying message being this is the right way, and unfortunately, the "right way" came from so many different forms that I would have been resistant as well. The westerners that came to support in the education reform came from different regions of the world, and so, of course, there were multiple interpretations of what was the right way. There were educational leaders from United States, South Africa, Ireland, New Zealand, Australia, United Kingdom, and more, and everyone thought their way was the right way. So, when I enter the building after four years into the program, and the natives have been exposed to what they may interpret as oppressive, dominating, and demeaning leadership support, they were going to be understandably resistant. I remember seeing one of the leaders walking down the hallway towards me, and when she looked up and saw me coming in her direction, she turned around and walked the other way. In the beginning, during leadership meetings, my help clearly wasn't wanted. This team I was charged in leading upward hadn't experienced a westerner on their staff; their knowledge was derived from their native colleagues that were further along in the program, where they were just starting. So, it wasn't like they had experienced the oppression, but they were certainly preparing themselves by being defensive. I continued to smile and offer small pieces of advice that were ignored. I watched as they struggled to operate the school. It wasn't that they couldn't do it; it was that the education reform brought drastic changes that they just weren't familiar with. For example, the size of the schools exceeded what they were accustomed to by three times. They were used to schools having 600 students, where there were now 1800. All of the small intimate schools that they were used to were, combined together making huge institutions.

These new buildings were multileveled with state-of-the-art technology, and many of the buildings also had swimming pools. With some of the new buildings came western principals, replacing the native leaders and sending them into early retirement. So, the leaders were fearful of losing their role in their community. To exasperate the notion further, the native parents embraced the western leaders, seeing them as more knowledgeable and more contemporary than their own people.

I could easily empathize with them; I can see how they were being made to feel that they were incapable, how others were better than them. I had felt those emotions several times in my life, and I didn't want to be the cause of their sorrow. But the truth of the matter was they were indeed failing, and they needed support. How was I to address their failure while maintaining their dignity? I watched for the areas where they struggled the most. I observed and tried to decipher how they processed and took action. It was difficult because I couldn't understand the language, and that was basically my problem; no one was offering translation. In the following meetings, I decided to bring in a tangible solution to one of their problems. It was undeniably an easy resolution to their problem. They couldn't refute it. I offered it humbly and told them as best as I could that I came to a conclusion by listening to and watching them, so it was, in fact, them who inspired my actions. It was, in fact, teamwork. That was the beginning of a great relationship with the principal of the school. I simply had to show her over and over again that I truly was a support for her and that I didn't want to demean her or take over her school. I was able to win the affection and trust of ninety-nine percent of the leadership team as well as all the teachers and students because I was empathetic, non-threatening, and was able to lead upwards. Most importantly, I was determined to be successful. Although I was placed in a completely unfamiliar environment with obstacles galore, I was determined not to give up, not to fail. I knew I could overcome the obstacles as long as I continued to put one foot in front of the other. But my natural response to stress, obstacles, and fear was to run, so I had to fight the urge to jump on a plane and travel back to the land of familiarity, where I knew I could succeed, as I had proven myself triumphant time and time again. I had to reach down and pull up the fighter in me, the same fighter who overcame obstacles as a child. I had to continue to shape who I was to become. I was still young, with dreams and aspirations; I had to persevere and continue to develop into the person I was called to be.

Activity Part II—*My Character Traits*

Of course, we know that I was deeply impacted by the teasing and oppression during my childhood. I felt as if I was a complete outcast. I hated my appearance and would do anything to change who I was so that I could fit into the image that was more accepted. I spent quite a bit of time alone, in a broken state. People that were supposed to support me, protect me, and encourage me, did the opposite. Teachers ignored the fact that I was being bullied. Family judged me for my mistakes. And those that were entrusted with my safety and protection robbed me of my innocence. I had a very difficult time trusting. When I was pregnant, I was basically discarded, and my boyfriend continued to explore other relationships. I felt unworthy of love and friendship. I have only touched the tip of the iceberg with the obstacles in my life. That wasn't the only incident of sexual abuse. That wasn't the only incident of physical abuse. That wasn't the only experience of abandonment. I hope you can see that life wasn't easy. I know there are some out there who can relate to my experiences. Receiving the love from my mother and my favored uncle was a great counter-experience to the pain and trauma I dealt with in life. Seeds of love and worthiness were planted and were my saving grace, but the noise of the world, more often than not, drowned out the positivity. A lot of what I experienced during my childhood; I carry with me today. It shaped me, just as the experiences I endured in pursuing my career shaped me. What I have shared in this book is a fraction of what has shaped me into the woman I am today, but hopefully, I've shared enough so far that you can see you are not alone in your struggles. And more importantly, I pray that you are receiving some messages to support you in this journey of life. I wish someone would have told me some of the things I am sharing with you. I wish someone would have shared with me a list of character traits in which to identify my current state of being when I was around twelve years old, just as we will do in our next activity. I would have liked to look at those adjectives and see if they reflected positivity, joy, resilience, and perseverance. I would have liked to know that my development was moving in a healthy direction, and if it wasn't, identify new, healthy character traits that I can aspire to possess. Parents, it's okay to share the character traits listed below with your children; start young and teach them self-reflection. It is only once we self-reflect that we can modify or adjust and grow.

Let's take a look at where we are now. I want you to select ten positive traits and at least five negative traits. As much as we would like to believe, we all have negative qualities. In order to gain an accurate sense of self, it is important that you are absolutely honest with yourself; no one is going to see it anyway! You can highlight them, circle them, or put tick marks; it's up to you. The highlights you see reflected in the chart are my choices.

Character Traits – Select 10 positive, at least 5 not-so-positive, and 5 aspirations.

Mine are identified below; I am doing this with you!

Afraid	Angry	Artistic	Athletic
Awesome	Beautiful	Bold	Awkward
Balanced	Bossy	Brilliant	Busybody
Self-Control	Careful	Charming	Cheerful
Confident	Dishonest	Disrespectful	Embarassed
Faithful	Exciting	Fair	Fearful
Foolish	Friendly	Fun	Funny
Generous	Gentle	Giving	Gredy
Grouchy	Happy	Helpful	Honest
Imaginative	Intelligent	Jealous	Kind
Lazy	Unmotivated	Lonely	Loving
Loyal	Lucky	Mean	Messy
Nervous	Nice	Nosy	Polite
Poor	Proud	Pretty	Love
Joy	Peace	Patience	Good
Quick	Quiet	Reserved	Outgoing
Respectful	Responsible	Rude	Sad
Selfish	Serious	Shy	Silly
Smart	Sneaky	Spoiled	Strict
Stubborn	Sweet	Talented	Terrified
Thankful	Thoughtful	Trusting	Doubtful
Suspicious	Worried	Patient	Wise
Wild	Talented	Clumsy	Brave
Unwise	Sluggish	Anxious	Untrustworthy
Standoffish	Energetic	Resilent	Persistent

My Choices—Character Traits

Ten Positive: Giving-Quiet-Careful-Resilient-Faithful-Persistent-Thankful-Patient-Polite-Fun

Five Not So Positives: Shy-Suspicious-Serious-Anxious-Reserved-Jealous

Five Aspirations: Wise-Bold-Calm-Controlled-Balanced-Energetic

Now, let's be honest, was it hard to select the not-so-nice character traits? And was it difficult to narrow down the positive ones! There are just so many positive attributes to choose from! Although I may sound a bit sarcastic right now, I am being quite serious. It really took me some time to complete this activity! I wanted to be absolutely honest with myself so that when I create my five-year goals at the end of this chapter, I am sure to make personal growth. If I am not honest here, I am only cheating myself from growth.

Before we move on to the next activity, I want you to read this Scripture. In this Scripture, there are many negative character traits. I want you to see if you have identified any of these in the traits you selected above. As you continue with the Scripture, the negative character traits are followed by traits that God refers to as the fruit of the spirit. Do you have any of these? Please do not go back and change any of your answers. Embrace the person that you initially depicted that you are. Then, we will work towards enhancing our positive attributes. If you remember my list, you will know that I am guilty of having negative character traits, but praise God, He is a forgiving Father. He knows the desires of my heart and will continue to help me work towards becoming the person He made me to be. He will work with you too if you just trust Him!

> Now the practices of the sinful nature are clearly evident: they are sexual immorality, impurity, sensuality (total irresponsibility, lack of self-control), idolatry, sorcery, hostility, strife, jealousy, fits of anger, disputes, dissensions, factions [that promote heresies], envy, drunkenness, riotous behavior, and other things like these. I warn you beforehand, just as I did previously, that those who practice such things will not inherit the kingdom of God. But the fruit of the Spirit [the result of His presence within us] is love [unselfish concern for others], joy, [inner] peace, patience [not the ability to wait, but how we act while waiting], kindness, goodness, faithfulness, gentleness, self-control. Against such things there is no law.

Galatians 5:19-23 (AMP)

When you look at this Scripture, did you find that any of your listed character traits align with the fruit of the spirit? If you did, that's fabulous! You are well on your way to becoming the person God intended you to be. For those of us who may not have identified characteristics from the fruit of the spirit, don't fret. We are going to create a plan to start moving in that direction, and with the help of God, we too will spend more time in the fruit of the spirit than giving in to our sinful nature, as we see depicted above in Scripture. But in order to grow, we must first be sure we have an accurate sense of self.

Activity Part III—*How Others See Me Shapes My Perception*

How important is it for you to be liked or respected? Do people see you as enjoyable, agreeable, easy-going, and understanding? Have you heard that you are attentive, patient, and open to new ideas? If so, good for you, as these are the common attributes of well-liked people. Do people see you as admirable, strong, having integrity, empathy, self-awareness, and influence? Are you known to be empathetic, brave, articulate, and honest? Can you admit you are wrong and avoid making excuses for your shortcomings? Are you known to be open to change and always seeking to better yourself? These are common attributes aligned with a person that is respected. Do people see you as a person who solves problems, a mediator, unbiased? Are you known to foster a positive culture and build strong relationships? Are you known as a visionary? Can you guide or direct people to accomplish common goals? Are you focused and self-confident as well as enthusiastic and humble? These are the common attributes of a successful leader.

How people see us is one of the major influencers of how we see ourselves. This activity is about how people see you. Many of these attributes may be identified in activities I and II. The most difficult part of the activity may be really thinking about your childhood and identifying the common themes that come to mind, and being honest with yourself. But keep in mind, it is important to reflect on our childhood, for it is during childhood that we start to shape our sense of self, and one of the ways we do that is through our interpretations of how others see us; we are specially shaped by the opinions of the influential adults in our life, followed by our peers. Examples of these influential people are parents or caregivers, close relatives, teachers, pastors, youth counselors, and babysitters. This is followed by peers or people we are around during most of our day, like friends and even their parents. If during childhood, we heard negative comments about ourselves, we may not want to experience reliving those times, but I guarantee that at the end of this chapter, we will be placed on a path of healing.

Like before, I will go first, reflecting on my childhood, young adulthood, and then reflecting on how people see me as a professional in my workplace. You have heard much of this already, but for the sake of the exercise, I will repeat it.

As a child, I often heard that I was ugly, bug-eyed, and very unattractive. I was told I had dark undesirable skin, and I was often discarded, chosen last, or ignored all together. I was withdrawn. Because I was sexually abused, I was broken-spirited and introverted and often felt unclean, dirty. One of the major themes as it pertains to my childhood, and the aftermath of it that creeps into my adult life, was that I was repulsive and unwanted. The adults in my life (in school) added to these perceptions because they did not correct the teasing or offer any comfort. But in contrast, I was athletic and resilient. I was agile yet sharp and precise. I was limber and fast. I enjoyed the outdoors, and I was adventurous. I didn't let bumps and bruises slow me down. So, another major theme in my childhood was that I was durable-strong. We don't recognize it, but there are always positives that go alongside the negatives. So, when you do your reflection, capture everything, the good and the not so good. This is how we start to change our negative self-perception. As a child, I couldn't see the good; I was drowned in the negative. The negativity I experienced shaped me more than anything; I didn't know to tap into the positive to create a healthier sense of self.

As a young adult, I was told that I would be a failure. I was told that I'd be a statistic, a drop-out, unsuccessful. I was abandoned by people that I loved and trusted, and I was made to feel unworthy. I was looked down upon, and I often wanted to be invisible. In contrast, I felt unconditional love from my mother. She always wanted me, and so did God, but at the time, I didn't know how to access His love.

As I entered adulthood and began my education and career, I was often celebrated for my hard work, commitment, determination, and ambition. I was seen as strong; I was respected and admired. I was also personable and patient, and although quiet and quite introverted, I was pleased to be around. I was resilient and optimistic and able to bring people to a consensus. Most people appreciated my directness and found me to be authentic and trustworthy. I was told I had a command presence, and although I didn't see myself that way, it showed itself to be true time and time again.

In summary, who we are as a person is derived from the negative *and* positive experiences we have in life. As a child, I felt that I was ostracized, visibly unpleasant, yet durable and resilient. As a young adult, I was abandoned, yet I was determined, committed, and resilient; and throughout my career, I was celebrated for being dedicated, productive, dependable, genuine, and compassionate. I was personable and admired. I was highly effective, respected considered to have a command presence. Ultimately, I was seen as a distinguished leader. I couldn't have been that leader without my childhood experiences. Being ostracized actually helped me to deal with the isolation as a school leader. School leaders are often alone, having to maintain the professionalism necessary to lead, evaluate and sometimes reprimand, while teachers are able to create bonds of friendship. My resiliency, determination, and commitment as a leader were derived from the pain of being told that I would be nothing in life and my relentless effort to prove people wrong. As I reflect on my past, I realize that I am ultimately created by *all* the experiences of my life. To bring about healing, I need to believe in the positive attributes and recognize that I am not a sum of the negative. I remember the good. I have positive experiences, I experienced love, and that is what I need to focus on. Because I have had pain, trauma, and scars on my past, the enemy will use that to negatively impact my present and future. But we must not let him! When you begin to have negative thoughts about yourself, immediately focus on a positive one, get out of the boxing ring with the devil, he doesn't deserve to be in our presence, ever!

I hope as you reflected on your life, you were able to capture the positives alongside the things that may have been troubling and recognize that we are shaped by all our experiences. I understand that when we have experienced lots of pain in life, we often don't recognize that there was also good; I hope you can see that now. I hope this was an eye-opening experience for you and that you can identify and celebrate the good.

Perception

Before we look at the result of our activity so far, I would like to talk about perception. I have made three different categories. As we look at the three types of self-perceptions, keep in mind to stay true to who you are. If you find that you identify with an area that may be depicted as harsh or distasteful in the descriptions, don't be discouraged. I am revealing to you what I have found as the three most common depictions of self-conception. Just be honest with yourself. This is all about you, your healing, and your growth.

We typically fall into three different categories when it comes to self-perception. Some people don't like looking at themselves closely, it can be uncomfortable, and so it is often avoided. Most of the time, it's because what is observed is not seen as desirable, and it's been that way for so long that they have accepted it. This category is called Self-Avoidance/Self-Hatred. Those in this group don't like what they see; they don't think they can change anything, so they often choose not to reflect. They are quiet and often withdrawn. Even when invited to engage with others, they find reasons not to. How did they get this way?

The next group is just the opposite; they are almost obsessed with self-reflection and self-opinion. They see themselves as wonderful and perfect. They strive for greatness; the more they reflect, the more they strive to be better, and the more their self-perception is shaped to exalt themselves. They are always in competition with themselves or others. They are in-tuned with the latest trends and must always be one of the first to experience a new fad, be it a piece of clothing, a new piece of technology, or anything that is popular. These people are high energy and are often the life of the party; they absolutely must be; they feel their best when the spotlight is on them. This group, we call Self-Exalting. How did they get this way?

The last group isn't popular or unpopular. They are known and accepted by most. They are not overly energetic, nor are they dull or boring. They maintain their composure quite easily, but they certainly laugh when things are funny and cry when they are sad. They are not unhealthily competitive and never compare themselves with others for greatness, but they do see and appreciate positive qualities in others, and they may strive to obtain those qualities. They offer accolades to others who earn it and support for those who need encouragement. They don't like the spotlight and would rather slide under the radar than be the center of attention. In fact, when given an applause, they will often include others in the praise. This group we will call, Self-Rectitude. How did they get this way?

Look below; how do you find yourself amongst this spectrum? One thing to understand about these three depictions of self-perception is they are not concrete. In fact, you may be somewhere in the middle of the three or have a combination of two. Most often than not, we can closely identify with one.

Self-Perception

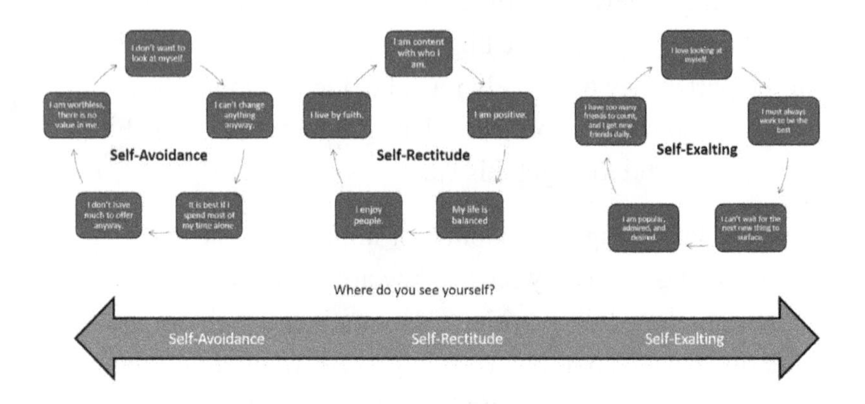

So, the question at the end of each description is, how did we get this way? The answer, we are shaped by our life experiences. We are shaped by how others see us. We are shaped by our actions or lack thereof. Our actions are shaped by our experiences. Our attitudes or opinions are shaped by our experiences *and* the result of our actions. Our motivations are shaped by our attitudes, which are shaped by our experiences

What if I told you there is a completely different way to perceive yourself? And what if I told you this way will bring you so much joy, relief, energy, and satisfaction? And, what if I told you it is so easy to obtain? It only requires one thing, to believe in something you cannot see. It requires faith. I wish someone would have told me; I don't have to be shaped by my self-perception, my life experiences, and how others see me. I wish someone would have told me, all I needed to do is believe in the Father, the Savior, the Lord, Jesus Christ. I wish I would have known that through faith in the Lord and a relationship with Him, I would come to see myself so differently than how the world sees me. I wish I would have known that my good works actually don't depict my worth. In fact, our Father in Heaven is so good, so faithful, and so merciful that He discards our good works as proof of our character or as a mandate for His love, mercy, and grace. In fact, He says in Ephesians 2:8-9 (ESV), "For by grace you have been saved through faith. And this is not your own doing; it is the gift of God, not a result of works, so that no one may boast."

Now you may say, how do you trust, believe and receive affirmation from having faith in God? How do you believe in something you can't see, touch, or feel? Well, once you accept God as your Lord and Savior, you are blessed with the Holy Spirit who will dwell inside you. The Holy Spirit fills you with God's presence. You will indeed *feel* His love and acceptance with a certainty that you have never experienced in your life. He will forgive your sins and release you from everything that holds you in bondage. If you only have faith in Him, your soul will be healed, and if you feel you are not broken, you will still experience an unexplainable freedom, an indescribable joy. He will reveal His plans for your life. Your eyes will see as never before. But know, our God is a God of freedom. He is not a controlling God, as some may think. We are so free that we get to choose our path. We get to choose whether or not to follow Him. We choose whether or not we want to live in His mercy and grace. We decide if we want to walk in the fruit of the spirit, accessing our true gifts and talents and using them to glorify Him. Only you can decide. Look at the illustration below and compare it with the one above. Wouldn't it be great to be released of the confinements of the illustration above and wallow in the freedom, love, and mercy of God? I have relinquished my life to God. Now I live by the illustration below. The world and the people in it do not dictate my character and my worth.

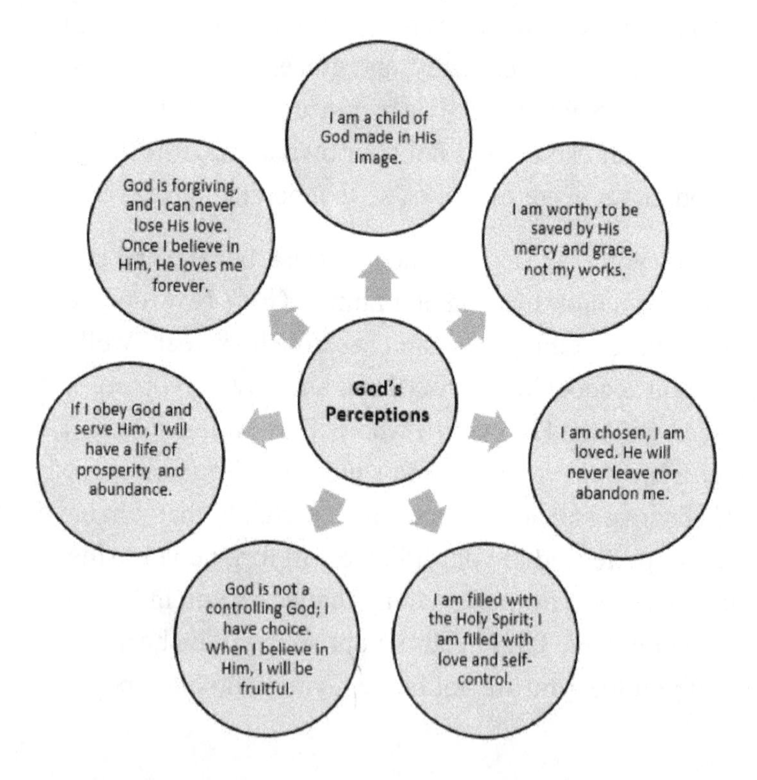

How fabulous it is to see myself as He sees me. How awesome it is that it doesn't depend on any other human being in this world. How awesome it is to know that when I walk in His light, stringing to live by the fruit of the spirit, I am the closest I will ever be to peace, joy, and fulfillment. It is so relieving to know that when I walk in His light, He will guide my path, showing me the direction I should go, revealing His plan for my life. How awesome to know that the confusion of life can be gone? And what a glorious concept to comprehend, that I don't need the acceptance or affirmation of the people of the world; that I am already accepted and loved. I wish someone would have told me! I wish I would have known all of this; then, I would have taken the time to enjoy my career, bathing in His acceptance and love, accessing my natural talent to lead, rather than striving to demonstrate my ability. I wish someone would have told me what I have just shared with you.

Let's stop and ponder all of this. Let's recap the activities of this chapter before we engage in our final activity and create our five-year plan. In Activity I, we engaged in self-reflection to give us a clear idea of how we became to be who we are today. We recaptured all our experiences from childhood to adulthood. In Activity II, we looked at the character traits that we would use to describe who we are today. We selected ten positive traits and five not-so-nice traits. Next, we selected five trait aspirations. Before we moved to the next activity, we were introduced to the fruit of the spirit and compared ours to the character traits that are in the Bible. Then we moved on to Activity III, in which we needed to reflect on how people see us. We know that how people see us is a major contributing factor to how we see ourselves. Then we looked at the typical three categories of self-perception and placed ourselves on the spectrum. We are getting a holistic view of how we have come to be who we are today. We finally ended activity III by having a look at God's perception of us. Isn't it fabulous to end on a positive note! To God be the glory!

ACTIVITY IV—*A LOOK IN THE MIRROR*

I want us to take a look in the mirror now. Yes, actually take a look in the mirror. Consider all the activities we have been through together and look long and hard at yourself. I want you to speak to yourself as if you were speaking to a stranger, so be sure to be alone; we don't want people to think we are crazy! Now, thinking about the activities, introduce yourself to yourself. Explain who you are and how you came to be. Explain how people see you? Answer the big question, do you agree with them? Affirm your view by sharing the character traits that you have identified for yourself. Now share what you have come to know about God's perception of you, and finally, share your aspirations. We will use your aspirations to create our five-year plan. As before, I will do this with you. You are not alone!

INTRODUCING DR. MONIQUE KAMMER

My name is Dr. Monique Kammer, and I want to share how I came to be who I am today. I am the second of four children. The only girl. My father passed away when I was eleven years old, so I was primarily raised by my mother, who loved me very much. My childhood was a mixture of good and bad, although, for many years, I felt the bad outweighed the good, so I didn't recognize the good. I was teased horribly as a child. Most of the teasing came from my appearance. I was seen as a very dark-skinned unattractive child, and I was ostracized because of it. In elementary, I felt better when I was alone in school, which was okay because the students made me feel alone anyway. They selected me last for sports and activities or basically made me feel invisible. The teacher rarely corrected their bad behavior, so I didn't have must trust in them. To make matters worse, during elementary years, I was sexually abused by those I trusted. The abuse went on for quite some time and was disguised as a game. As I became a bit older, I experienced sexual abuse by men outside my family on two other occasions. It made me even more of an introvert. I was quite confused about it all and carried that confusion into my adult life. But I was also a very strong little girl. I took karate classes throughout my youth, and that taught me how to be limber and agile, yet strong and sturdy. It was one of the reasons I was so good at cheerleading and the drill team. I was actually great at it! Even though I was denied the opportunity to be a cheerleader in high school because of my appearance. This denial, of course, contributed to my negative self-perception. But I persevered! I became the captain of the drill team and still enjoyed the year and a half that I was in high school. High school was short-lived because I had a baby at the age of sixteen. When the school found out that I was pregnant, they sent me away to a school for pregnant girls. They said I would be a statistic, that I would ultimately be a dropout. I didn't know what they meant at the time; I just know it didn't feel good. There was one person that told me that I could still be whatever I wanted to be in life. That my current situation was only an obstacle and that if I overcome the obstacle, I would be just as successful as the next person. The baby's father and I were not successful. He was young and naturally interested in living his life rather than being a father. So, I felt abandoned. To go along with that, one of my most favored uncles also abandoned me. He told me that he would do nothing for me, ever. That he would support my child, but not me. He was disappointed in me and hurt. The pain and rejection I felt from that conversation, coupled with the encouragement from my counselor, was ultimately what motivated me to strive for greatness. I attended night school and received my General Education Diploma. After that, I enrolled in the junior college, and guess what? I was a cheerleader! I also ran for homecoming queen and was able to experience the same events I would have if I had gone to high school, it was fabulous, but it was also a distraction. I spent a bit too much time at the junior college; I was more interested in the activities and fun than my studies. But I was able to experience a great friendship. We were inseparable for years. We had so much in common! We just clicked! We inspired each other; we held each other accountable. We secured our first steady job as bus drivers, which would ultimately see us through college and open up the doors to becoming teachers. Then one day, our friendship ended. She felt we just weren't close anymore. I was again abandoned and broken-hearted. It fed my self-perception of not being worthy of love and friendship. But I persevered. I became a teacher and was good at it! Actually, I was great! I worked so hard to be there for my students! They meant the world to me. I wanted to be the teacher that I never had. That hard work was noticed, and I was encouraged to become the Activities Director of a very large high school. There were over 3500 students. I excelled in the role of activity director. I received accolades from my immediate colleagues as well as the Superintendent of Schools. My mentors told me I was a hardworking, dedicated educator. They said I possessed the necessary skills to become an administrator. They recognized that I was great with students, teachers, and parents. They said I was great at building relationships and managing people. It was interesting because I never saw myself that way. I knew I was a fighter. I knew that I had perseverance. But I felt so shy. In fact, I hated speaking in front of people in a large crowd, which I found myself often doing. I was terrified every time. Somewhere along my time as an educator, I found a new best friend. And again, we were inseparable. Although I was always quite suspicious of people and didn't know how to trust, I loved her deeply. She was the sister I never had. Also, during my career, I married. I thought I would be married for my entire life, but he felt that I wasn't enough and cheated on me. I was again broken and had now taken on the trait of jealousy. I was insecure in every relationship. I adopted a serious demeanor. So, I wasn't just shy anymore. I was shy and serious. I have often been told to smile! Why are you looking so serious? I didn't even realize I was stone-faced. I was just always on guard. I suppose that is where the command presence came from. Although my teachers often told me that they were initially afraid of me. I was intimidating; once they got past the barrier, the wall of protection, they can still see that timid little girl. My career moved fast. I became an assistant principal and principal, and before you knew it, I had graduated my kids from school and sent them to college. They ended up taking their own path in life, but I got them there. It all went by in a blur! I was chasing success! It felt great. It made me feel worthy, powerful, successful. Ultimately, I moved to the other side of the world, to the Middle East, where I would support them in education reform. My best friend came with me. My experience there was quite like my experience in the States. Although it was a huge challenge with many obstacles, I was very successful. I was able to lead a staff successfully of people who didn't even speak my language. I had other failed relationships, and a huge wedge was placed between my best friend and me. She had to return to the States, and I chose to stay in the Middle East a bit longer. Perhaps that is where the breakdown started to happen. Excruciating heartbreak again. But eventually, I was blessed with a loving, gentle and supportive husband. That is when the biggest change happened in my life. My spirit and drive for life became broken. I was restless and couldn't find peace. I wanted to chase after my broken friendship; I wanted to be closer to my children, I missed my family terribly. We couldn't figure it out, but I just wasn't fulfilled. Eventually, we returned to the States. But my job was unfulfilling. My family had continued life without me. Although a bit unstable, they were surviving without their matriarch. The friendship is there but has lost its depth. Even back in the States, I was not fulfilled. I couldn't secure a satisfying job in education, no matter how hard I tried.

One day, my husband and I decided I should quit my job and rest. I had begun to suffer some unidentifiable illnesses and was in pain quite a bit. We thought maybe if I were to just be still, we could hear God talk to me. We went to church regularly, and we tried with all our might to keep God in the center of our marriage. But I wasn't experiencing God. I had been so busy throughout my life chasing success and acceptance that I completely lost connection with God. He has always been there, and trust me; He revealed Himself to me time and time again. But I thanked Him for picking me up and setting me straight, and then I was off again in the race of life! I am sure there were times that I didn't even thank Him! But He faithfully carried me when I called His name. He calmed my soul and rebuilt my strength. He is why I persevered. Funny, all this time I thought it was me!

Once I was still and heard God calling to me, He calmed my spirit completely. Gave me direction and purpose again. He told me I would continue to teach, but it wouldn't be in public education. He told me I would lead, but it wouldn't be a group of school administrators. He had a different calling for me, all together! Something I would have never imagined. All this time, He had been preparing me to do the work that He had in store for me. So now I have new aspirations. I aspire to be wise in His Word so that I can minister to those in need. I was told to be bold in my belief so that I had the confidence to proclaim His Word. He tells me to be calm and controlled and that I can find these attributes as I continue to build my relationship with Him. He is the purpose of my life. He is the reason I breathe. I needed to switch up some things and find balance, and through that, I have a new and restored energy.

I know what I want to be doing in five years. What about you? When you spoke to yourself about your life and how you came to be who you are today, were you enlightened? When you captured all those character traits in your explanation of self, were your eyes opened? You were explaining your self-perception. You were telling yourself who you are and how you came to be that way.

When you reflected on God's perception of you, how did you feel? Let's take a moment to do that again. Go to the diagram of God's Perception and read all the bubbles. Isn't it great to see that the only love and acceptance you need is His, and you already have it! So, let me tell you, stop chasing! Let's think about how we can put the brakes on and recenter ourselves. How do we want to grow in the next five years? Let's pray about it first and then make our plan.

Prayer

My Heavenly, Sovereign Father,

I want to thank You for my life, all of it, Lord, the good and the not so good. Lord, the Bible tells me there will be trials and tribulations in my life, in everyone's life. I understand that, Father, and in all the trials I have experienced, Lord, You fought for me, and took me out of the fire, every single time; and I am forever grateful. Lord, Exodus 14:4 tells me that You will always fight for me, I only have to be silent. Lord, I had a troubled spirit, and once I was still enough to hear You, Lord, You spoke to me. You have a plan for my life, You always have. But I've been busy doing my own thing. Lord, thank You for Your patience and the freedom You have given me to choose my path. I know now that my journey so far has been to prepare me to do the work You are calling me to. At one point I thought I would reach the ultimate satisfaction that life had to offer, but I would have never found that fulfilment. In fact, I was pretty run down and exhausted. Lord, it is only when I was still that I could hear You calling me, showing me what I was to do. And Father, I'm sorry I started running. I didn't believe, I could be worthy of spreading the love and Word of God. But You have shown me otherwise. In fact, Lord, You have shown me that I am most happy and at peace when I am studying Your Word and writing, using my life to show others how Your grace and mercy have made me what I am today. I am victorious through sexual abuse, oppression, physical abuse, and sadness because You brought me through the fire, every time circumstances or choices put me in it. And Lord, all of it was to prepare me to be of service to You. Lord, lead me, I surrender. I am done chasing approval from the world. Thank You, Father, for loving me as I am. Thank You for seeing me as worthy. Lord, words cannot express my gratitude and love for You, so I am thankful You know my heart. Lord, I hear Your call, father guide me as I make my five-year plan. Lord, I want You at the center of whatever I do. Time has taught me that only then, I am most at peace and fulfilled. I thank You in advance Lord, in Jesus's name I pray, Amen and Amen.

Yes! Now let's make our plan. As you know, I am an educator and former trainer of education administrators. We lived by what is known as a SMART plan. What the acronym smart stands for is specific, measurable, achievable, relevant, and timely. So, we, too, will use the well-known SMART plan for our goals, but with a little twist. Let's start by selecting three goals.

Think about your past experiences. Think about your character traits and the things you want to aspire to be. I think I will select two things that I want to aspire for and one thing to let go of. Feel free to select as many things as you wish, but I caution you to go beyond five goals. These goals need to be in our face daily, and if they become too heavy, we will walk away, and we are trying to do away with self-defeating tendencies! So only bite off what you can chew. Let's use this template to complete our goals. You will need to recreate it so that everything fits for you. Like before, I will enter my first one here, as your guide.

The Specific Goal: Is it God-centered? How can you make it?		How to measure growth?	Is it achievable; how do you know? Be reminded by listing it here.	Is the goal realistic? Reflect about the reality of it here.	At what point do you want each goal to be accomplished? What will your next steps be? We are always growing!
1	Complete the *Messages to Those Who Come After Me* book series.	The publication of at least one book each year.	It is achievable, I feel this is calling by God, and I believe that I can do all things through Christ who strengthens me.	The goal is realistic. I have stopped working a regular job to commit myself to my writing. It is my job.	I should publish at least one book every year. Next steps, use my books to give lectures and seminars. Perhaps serving as a weekend retreat for women.
2					
3					

As you can see, these are big goals! So, don't choose too many of them. I would love for you to share your experiences with me. You can email me at **mlk@mymessage-sministries.net.** I would love to share the journey with you.

I would like to leave you with the Scriptures that I use when I face trials and tribulations or when I doubt my worth. I hope you, too, will find peace and comfort as you read them through a troubled time.

- If you are discouraged by your life's circumstances, review the Scriptures below.

> Count it all joy, my brothers, when you meet trials of various kinds, for you know that the testing of your faith produces steadfastness. And let steadfastness have its full effect, that you may be perfect and complete, lacking in nothing. If any of you lacks wisdom, let him ask God, who gives generously to all without reproach, and it will be given him. But let him ask in faith, with no doubting, for the one who doubts is like a wave of the sea that is driven and tossed by the wind.

James 1:2-8 (ESV)

> "Do not be anxious about anything, but in everything by prayer and supplication with thanksgiving let your requests be made known to God. And the peace of God, which surpasses all understanding, will guard your hearts and your minds in Christ Jesus".

Philippians 4:6-7 (ESV)

> "And we know that for those who love God all

things work together for good, for those who are called according to his purpose".

Romans 8:28 (ESV)

"When the righteous cry for help, the LORD hears and delivers them out of all their troubles. The LORD is near to the brokenhearted and saves the crushed in spirit".

Psalm 34:17-18 (ESV)

"Have I not commanded you? Be strong and courageous. Do not be frightened, and do not be dismayed, for the LORD your God is with you wherever you go" .

Joshua 1:9 (ESV)

"But God, being rich in mercy, because of the great love with which he loved us, even when we were dead in our trespasses, made us alive together with Christ—by grace you have been saved".

Ephesians 2:4-5 (ESV)

Key Message

Our character begins to form from a small child. We are born with our own distinct talents, and genetics also play a role in who we become, but we are primarily shaped by our life experiences. From the first hug we experienced to the first reprimand. We began to understand love and discipline. From the rules and structure from our youth to the friends we hang around and the teachers who taught us. All the experiences of life have had an impact on who we are today. We are like sponges soaking up all encounters, good and bad, joyful and tragic. Each and every one of them starts to shape our character. Every kind word, every accolade, attaboy, hug, high-five and kiss, fosters a sense of security, self-worth, encouragement, motivation, and a positive impact on our self-perception, and every harsh word, careless critique, repetitive teasing, every hit, smack, slap or punch tears us down physically as well as emotionally. Physical abuse, sexual abuse, and abandonment can ultimately destroy a person's sense of self-worth. We are literally shaped by our experiences. We deeply believe that we are whatever those character traits that we identified earlier say we are. If you have been blessed in a way that you have experienced minimal hardship, trust me, it is a blessing. But if you are like me and lived a life that had plenty of traumatic experiences, then your self-perception may not be healthy. But it doesn't have to stay that way because God's perception of us is all we need. And in order to share in His perception, you must do one thing, and that is to believe that our Lord and Savior sent His one and only Son as a sacrifice for our sins. We are then forgiven for all of our wrongdoings in the past, the present, and the future! Once you believe you are free from the bondage that held you captive, and you are gifted with God's mercy and grace, His healing, and love, you must only believe in His perception of you and walk in His light. Nothing else matters. Nothing! Yes, accolades and words of affirmation are great for our soul and spirit, and we should receive them humbly because there is really no need to be rewarded for walking in the spirit. We have to be careful of too many recognitions, less we adopt a self-exalting self-perception, and we don't want that. In fact, walking by the Spirit is in itself the greatest reward we can receive because it puts us in a direct relationship with the Father and helps us to resist the flesh. Galatians 5:16 (NASB) says, "But I say, walk by the Spirit, and you will not carry out the desire of the flesh." The close we are to God, the stronger we are against the enemy, the humbler we are, the more we reap the rewards promised to us in Scriptures. Walking in the spirit is still excelling in your job; it's still being recognized for your hard work, but then in return, you give God the praise because everything we do should be to glorify Him! So be humble. But be healed! Let go of the pain from your past and know that you are loved; you are beautiful, you are strong and courageous, you are a child of God. Let that shine in everything you do.

Now, let's finish what we started. How would you describe yourself in three sentences or less? My description of myself is, I am a leader. I excel and enjoy leading and teaching people. I aspire to use my talent to spread the Word of God to women of all ages.

Chapter Six: It's Okay to Start over Again, and Again, and Again

One of the most enjoyable things I did growing up as a child was to play games with my family. It was the best family time of all, filled with laughter and healthy competition. I remember playing games with my mom and my brothers as early as first and second grade. Being a mother of four young children can be expensive, so before we could afford to buy board games, my mom created her own games to play with us. One game I remember playing often was spelling competitions. My mom would give us a word to spell, and whoever got the word right would get a small animal cracker. We would play that game until the box of little animal cracker were gone! It didn't matter who won the game because we would start that game over the following day until we all mastered those words, and then guess what; there was a new list of words, so we would start the game over and over again. The game of spelling was never-ending in our youth because there were always new words for us to learn! I didn't realize it at the time, but we were practicing our spelling words from school!

Once I got older, another game I loved playing was monopoly. We would play that game for hours, and we took it quite seriously! Of course, we took it seriously; this game was like real life! We were playing with money, property, loans, taxes, chances, and possible jail time. It was all just a game, but we all wanted to be the winner. We wanted to become the wealthiest player on the board. We wanted to collect as much property as we could, and make as much money as we could, and force the other players to bankruptcy. This game would take hours, and after a quick celebration at the end, we would start it all over again. What a fantasy! When we were bankrupt, hit rock bottom, and pushed out of the game, all we had to do was wait a while and start all over again. We all tried to learn the best strategies to win, so when we started over, our chances of winning were more likely. Although we had to sit out and wait for the game to end, it was a good thing because we were able to watch closely and try to learn the winners' strategy so that we can be successful in the life of Monopoly.

Just like in the board games, we get to start over as many times as we need to in real life. We are made to believe that starting over makes a failure from our previous endeavors, but we couldn't be more wrong. We discussed in Chapter Four about being rationally resilient in our decision-making, and starting over in life is simply an extension of that resiliency. So, whether we are starting over because our first attempt at life didn't turn out the way we wanted it to, or whether we are starting a new career after a stint in another area, it is absolutely ok. If we have had a few hiccups in life that are causing us to start over, that's okay too, and if we have had epic failures in some areas, well, guess what, that just fine! You can start over in that area too. Remember from Chapter Two; we are exactly where we are supposed to be. So always embrace the blessed opportunity to start all over again.

I would have never thought that I would be seeking a new career as I approached fifty years old, but the Lord had a different plan for me. This new calling just didn't seem right for me, so I was doing everything I could to run from it. I wanted to continue in education. I was extremely resistant and actually disobedient. The thing is, I have started over time and time again in my past; it's just that it wasn't as blatant as this one. In this one, I literally had to veer off a clearly paved path and travel down a completely unknown road. Was I afraid? Absolutely, I was even ignoring the small still voice of God and still trying to seek my own way. Yet, every time I tried to travel down the familiar road, there were roadblocks of some kind. The roadblocks were unexplainable and made no sense. How could I not secure a job in education when I had the highest college degree in that area and a successful resume to boot. In fact, in every application I completed, I literally ticked all the boxes; I was sometimes overqualified. But I didn't get the favorable responses I expected. When I did get an opportunity to interview, for some reason, I was completely tongue-tied. I could not get my sentences to come out smoothly. I stumbled over words and was completely flustered. I found myself practicing for interviews, which really blew my mind because I have interviewed hundreds of candidates in my time; I know the questions, and I know the answers. Yet, the words wouldn't flow out of my mouth eloquently. I was embarrassed, sad, and felt so defeated. I was confused; I didn't understand. But I was resilient! I tried over and over again, determined to get a job in education. Finally, God said to be still! Then guess what? I received instructions on how to start over. You know this story, so I don't need to go into detail but know your Heavenly Father has a plan for you if you will only be still enough to listen. To help prepare you as you listen for His guidance, try to understand that you may be called to do something that you may think you cannot accomplish; you might think it is far beyond you, I did! I immediately started to doubt. I started to discredit myself, convince myself that I was not worthy of His calling. But He kept on calling because when you hear negativity creeping into your mind about a plan that your gut tells you have been sent by God, you can rest assured that it is not the Holy Spirit trying to talk you out of it. In fact, the Lord our God tells us not to fear, and since I love and trust God, I went all in, and so should you. God will equip you with what you need; you will not fail. The Bible teaches us in Luke 12:31 (NLT), "Seek the Kingdom of God above all else, and he will give you everything you need." So, when you are in doubt, go to God first. Pray, then move forward and trust that God will guide your steps. This is having faith. When you stumble pray, again. It's okay to start over again, and again, and again. In fact, evidence that God calls us to start over in life is seen when he selects His twelve disciples.

These men had no idea they were going to change direction, midlife. A story we are most familiar with when it comes to Jesus selecting His disciples was the story of Simon, called Peter, and his brother Andrew. The two of them were engaging in their daily trade of fishing when

Jesus sought them and encouraged them to follow him and become fishers of men. Without a moment's hesitation, they dropped what they were doing and followed. Just a bit later, Jesus recruited his next two disciples, James and John. They were working with their father, mending their fishing nets, when Jesus called them. They, too, immediately dropped what they were doing and walked away from not only their trade of fishing but their earthly father as well. The new disciples had no idea what they were getting themselves into, but that didn't deter them from following Jesus. They started life all over again. It was the same as the other disciples. Matthew was a Roman tax collector. To be a tax collector, one had to be educated. Thus, he also had a decent salary. Matthew had also turned away from the Jewish religion and kept the company of sinners. Matthew sought after wealth. He chased power and assets. But he threw it all away to start over for something that was obviously more important. When I think of Matthew, it reminds me that it doesn't matter what you have accumulated in life; when God calls, be willing to throw it all away to follow Him.

Perhaps, it may seem that starting over to follow God is not a fair comparison, but isn't it? The disciples dropped everything to follow Jesus, and if we find ourselves staring at a closed door and having to look in the direction of new possibilities in life, shouldn't we be seeking the support and guidance of God. People typically start over when they have hit rock bottom or hit glass ceilings in life. Usually, things are starting to come crashing down around us, or we can no longer see growth in our current situation. These are not your typical everyday life experiences. We are talking about life-altering moves that require the Decision-Making Process and the foundation of Christ. We are talking about decisions that totally change our lives and may impact other people's life as well. I feel confident in saying we will all have start-over moments in our life; some may be devastating, like death, divorce, an empty nest, or illnesses, all requiring us to start over in some way. Then there are more positive ones like the birth of a child, graduation from school or college, new marriages combining two families, new jobs, or even retirement. Starting over can certainly tug at our emotions, test our abilities and faith. Whether they are unexpected or predicted where you get to create a plan and strategically start again, whatever the case is, it's okay. You are exactly where you are supposed to be. In fact, starting over is creating life experiences, and we know that life experiences shape our character. We get to restore or refine who we are, bringing us more aligned to walking in the fruit of the spirit. Don't be discouraged; embrace each opportunity. I wish someone would have told me that every time I start over, brings me closer to my Heavenly Father.

When I started to think of areas where I've had to start over, I couldn't just select one topic to discuss with you. Several topics came to mind, and I want to share a few to really highlight how every time I started over, it was the right thing to do, and that in some way, it brought me closer to God. I also want to capture what would have been the alternative to starting over. Each start-over will contain Scripture(s) that fit the circumstance to really underscore my belief that God fits in every area of our life. We can seek His guidance and wisdom in everything we do.

- Start-over decision #1: Going back to school after dropping out.
- Start-over decision #2: Trusting intimate relationships after experiencing abuse, abandonment, and failure.
- Start-over decision #3: Mending the broken relationship with my son; helping him reset his life.

Reap What You Sow

After I had my daughter, I was blessed with assistance from the government. I received money as well as food stamps and medical assistance. For this, I was grateful. I truly had no idea of the responsibilities of having a child to care for. At sixteen years of age, I was barely learning how to take care of myself. Without government assistance, I would have been completely lost. My mother did what she could, but she was an incredibly young grandmother, and she still had her own life to live. With government support, I was able to pay the rent, buy groceries and visit the doctor when needed. Initially, it was comfortable. I hadn't made any other bills for myself, so it seemed that with rent paid and food on the table, everything was covered. I was so comfortable that I forgot about my goals and aspirations. I started hanging out and wasting my time. I was very unproductive. Nothing good came from my days. I was spending my time around other people that were not moving forward in life and not contributing to society yet receiving resources from the government. They were all capable young people, and so was I. Sadly, the more I was in unhealthy company, the more I became unmotivated and ineffective. Now, as I reflect on my past, I can clearly see the message of Proverbs 13:4 (NLT), "The soul of the sluggard craves and gets nothing, while the soul of the diligent is richly supplied." Here is a message for you; if you are capable of working and contributing to society, do so. If you are limited in your abilities, find something that you can do that is within your means. The reward of a productive life is more than monetary. You are rewarded in many ways. You gain skills such as teamwork, communication, problem-solving, adaptability, and sometimes leadership skills. If your work requires you to help others, you learn to build empathy. Being productive in work or school also helps you to develop a positive work ethic, and your contribution to society helps you to develop a positive sense of identity. When I think of being a productive person, I am reminded of 2 Corinthians 9:6 (KJV), "The point is this: whoever sows sparingly will also reap sparingly, and whoever sows bountifully will also reap bountifully." I often understood this Scripture as relating to money, but the truth is, sowing means to place a seed in the soil to germinate and grow. Every day we contribute our time and energy (our seed) into positive actions and behaviors; we are producing opportunities to grow, receive, or acquire positive rewards (reap). This was the reason we were created. To enrich the beauty of this world God created. Not to just sit and receive its beauty. For if we are idle, it can surely contribute to our death. Proverbs 12:27-28 (NOG) tells us, "a lazy hunter does not catch his prey, but a hardworking person becomes wealthy. Everlasting life is on the way of righteousness. Eternal death is not along its path." The path I was on was leading me in the wrong direction, and I am thankful that God opened my eyes to the importance of being productive and contributing to society. He clearly showed me that the money from welfare was not enough, that I was stagnant, and that I was capable of providing a better life for my child. I saw this as I walked down the busy road pushing a grocery basket full of food. I saw this when my car broke down and there was no extra money to fix it. I saw it the morning I awoke feeling miserable after an evening of drinking too much and hanging out. God was reprimanding me, and I knew better. I knew that there was another way. So, I committed to going back to school. I started over.

The Command to Love

How do you prepare a young person for the hurt they will undoubtedly experience in life from those they love? How do you prepare them to deal with the hurt from random people or situations? I am not talking about when you are chastised by a parent, and the hurt you feel is your own conviction. I am talking about the hurt you get from your first break-up or the hurt you get when you are teased mercilessly for things that are out of your control. Or sadly, I am talking about the hurt you get from being abused. I am talking about the hurt that happens when a friendship comes to an end or the hurt that happens when you are oppressed or experience any injustice. What do you do when you experience hurt over and over again, creating so much scar tissue that it is impossible to heal? Some may get angry, and some want to hurt the ones who hurt them. Some of us hold on to that pain and internalize it, trying to take the blame as a means to end the hurt. Some go into depression, and sadly some end their own lives. We are told in Scripture to "forget about the wrong things people do to you. You must not try to get even. Love your neighbor as you love yourself. I am the LORD" (Leviticus 19:17-19, ICB). But how do you teach a child how to do this. How do you teach a victim of abuse to forget about the wrongs people have done to them? It took me a very long time to learn how to let go, and unfortunately, sometimes, I am still momentarily impacted by hurt.

As you know, I was abused as a child by people that were close to me, as well as from strangers. I have also experienced abandonment and rejection from those I loved and trusted. As a young adult, I didn't know how to deal with the emotions that came from abuse, rejection, or abandonment. So, I became very guarded and introverted. It was difficult for me to trust. I was physically and emotionally scarred, and it was hard to let people in. When I add the relentless teasing I experienced growing up, you may get an idea of how difficult it was for me to trust people at all. I was always reluctant, even with those that were truly lovely people. I was suffering from fear of abandonment. I knew that ultimately, shutting people out of my life would cause me more harm, especially because I liked people. Harvesting hatred would have further imprisoned me. Continuing to isolate myself only added to those shackles. So, I chose to start over again. It wasn't easy. In fact, I experienced anxiety every time I am to engage with someone new on a personal level. When my husband and I signed up to join a Christian couples' small group, I was excited! Both of us had been praying to find a church, get involved, and meet other like-minded couples. The church we found was great, and we even started to serve on the First Impressions Team, but we hadn't been plugged into a group. When we received the call, we were both excited. The group leaders planned a potluck for our introductory meeting. I happily prepared one of my favorite side dishes and was ready to meet everyone until the day of the meeting. I became overwhelmed with anxiety, and we had to cancel. Solitude was safer. But I had to start again. I had to trust God. Whatever came of the new relationships was exactly as it should be. I had to keep that in mind that the people that we were about to meet would be in our life for a reason, a season, or a lifetime. This was something I prayed for. When we tried to join the group again, it was so rewarding! We really enjoyed the people in our small group, and now we consider each other family.

I wish someone would have told me early in life that to be prepared for the hurt that comes with relationships of all kinds. I wish I would have known not to take it personally when relationships came to an end. I wish I would have known to go through the process of healing when I experienced hurt from a loved one. Having built that capacity would have better equipped me to deal with the oppressions of the world. I wish I would have known that going through the cycle of healing when I was first abandoned or rejected would have given me the strength to simply wish the person well in life, appreciate the time I had with them, and move forward with minimal hurt feelings. It would have also helped me to deal with the natural rejections that come in life, for example, not being selected for a job.

In all things related to the hurt we experience from people we come across in life, the key message is not internalizing the situation, be it abuse, rejection, abandonment, or oppression. It is not your fault. Always be ready to start again to build positive relationships. We were made to fellowship. People will continue to enter and exit our life, be thankful and appreciate them for the time you have them. Let them go when it is time for them to leave. For those that hurt you with the wickedness of abuse or oppression, forgive. Trust me, I know it's tough. But you must forgive for your own freedom and grace. We are told that if "you do not forgive others their trespasses, neither will your Father forgive your trespasses." (Matthew 6:16, ESV)

I made the decision to love again, to forgive all who have wronged me in any way. If I don't forgive, my Father will not forgive me, and I need His forgiveness and grace. God gives us detailed instructions on how to live a healthy life, one that draws us to walk in the fruit of the spirit. We don't always have to understand or agree; we only have to live by faith and obey. We know that God is all-powerful and all-knowing. It is impossible for us to even imagine the splendor of his Glory. We must have faith and forgive and let go. Isaiah 55:8-9 (NIV) tells us that God says, "For my thoughts are not your thoughts, neither are your ways my ways, "declares the LORD. As the heavens are higher than the earth, so are my ways higher than your ways and my thoughts than your thoughts." Oh, how great is our God; you will experience immense peace if you just believe! I feel so much closer to God because I let go of the weight of harvesting negative feelings. My heart feels lighter, and my spirit is joyful. Now, I look at everyone through the eyes of love and grace, just as I want them to look at me.

Wayward Child

I am almost fifty years old, and there is still nothing like the comfort of my mother's hug, the soothing sound of her voice. I just love it when I walk into her house, and I get that old familiar, and comfortable smell of home. I now hear my children saying the same thing, and that is so reassuring to my soul. It is reassuring when I hear or see that they appreciate their upbringing and recognize the love that I gave them and that here in my arms is where they still find comfort. It's such a balancing act, offering the nurturing love of a mother to your children that are already adults. You have to respect their adulthood without being too overbearing and while simultaneously offering the support, encouragement, guidance, and motivation that they need. It is especially difficult when they are trying to recover from a road that you warned them not to go down in the first place. It is also heart-wrenching to have some sort of animosity between you and your child, creating a very strained relationship during a time of need. It is altogether worse to feel as if you have lost your child due to your own negligence. To exasperate matters, it is mindboggling when for a long time, you couldn't even see your errors; in fact, you felt as if you did everything right when you raised them and that it was their own decisions that have caused strife. How do you recover from such heartache? The child is now an adult. Do you remain cordial, having a surface-level relationship with your offspring, or do you start over again? Let me tell you what worked for me; I started over again!

I mentioned before that when my son graduated from high school, he went to the university, and I went to the Middle East. We agreed that I would stay a minimum of four years while he earned his bachelor's degree. In the midst of all the excitement of him graduating high school and going to college and me going abroad, there was no time for hesitations or worries. We were functioning on pure adrenaline. I admit I was wee a bit nervous about taking up my entire life to reside in a country that I was not familiar with at all, but my excitement drowned out the apprehension. I wasn't at all concerned with my son going to the university. School came easy to him, and he was one of the top graduates in his class. I knew for sure he would be successful. We regularly connected during the first semester. We skyped so I could see him in his dorm room and see that all was going well. But as you know, it wasn't. He was only successful for the first semester. After that, everything went downhill. He and his roommates were enjoying the freedom of adulthood without living up to the responsibilities. Of course, that came to an abrupt halt at the end of the year, when grades wouldn't allow them to continue living in the dorm. It was during that first semester that my son needed me most. That was a point where we could have discussed the obstacles and agreed on a path of correction. But I wasn't in the States. I am not exactly sure when things got so bad, but I can clearly remember one occasion of us yelling back and forth at each other, trying to identify who was responsible, and trying to express our hurt. He felt abandoned, and I felt he just didn't live up to his end of the deal. He felt like he couldn't reach out and touch me, and

I felt as if I were just a phone call away. Initially, I refused to take responsibility; but I quite often cried myself to sleep at night. It was heart-wrenching because my son and I were like two peas in a pod. After my divorce, it was just he and I in the home, and it remained that way throughout his middle school and high school years. We did everything together, camping, skiing, going on cruises, visiting colleges, you name it. It was always Mark and me! So, to have the slightest bit of tension between us was unacceptable, but to have a huge wedge between us was unbearable.

I rationalized on how I did the right thing as a mother. He was absolutely successful in high school, so why would I think twice about the university. My rationalization was confirmed by friends and family members, offering justification for my actions. Yet, his feelings were valid. His hurt stemmed from there being no one physically there for him. No one, being me. All the other friends had their mother. But I wasn't going to accept that I was the reason he was not successful; in fact, I wanted him to own his actions. He needed to learn how to recover from his mistakes. Doesn't the Bible say in Proverbs 13:24 (NIV), "whoever spares the rod hates his son, but he who loves him is diligent to discipline him"? It was very important for me to show my son that he needed to be responsible for the choices that he made. I wholeheartedly believed that and I still do, but I also had to acknowledge my mistakes. The first mistake that I made was that I didn't create a solid foundation in life for him. The foundation I am speaking about is Jesus. Like my upbringing, I took my son to church regularly. He went to his Sunday school classes and learned whatever the teacher or volunteer in children ministries taught him.

I asked him what he learned, and I made sure that he was able to articulate the message he got, but that was basically where it ended. We occasionally prayed aloud over our meals, but we never really prayed together outside of that. I failed to demonstrate that God was the center of my life because was he? Not really. My prayers were mostly during the highs and the lows. I prayed when things were great, and I prayed when I was broken and needed guidance; other prayers were randomly sprinkled throughout. I daily praised God through worship music; in fact, it was the genre of music most listened to when the kids were young. Other music had to be clean, just as their television programs had to be clean. They weren't free to watch what they wanted or listen to what they wanted. I know now that it only happened like this is in my presence. As they grew up, they were exposed to media in school. But I did my best to provide parental provisions. Unfortunately, what I provided was on the surface. I failed to show the importance of intentionally having God in our life every day. I failed at showing my kids how to seek him for guidance, support, and comfort. I failed to show them how to praise Him when He answered prayers, so they could recognize that He did answer prayers. I wish I would have taken the time to really teach my children about God. I am telling you what I wish someone would have told me, go beyond Sunday school and teach your children about God. Model what they should be doing as a faithful child of God. Talk to God in front of your children, be the example, plant the seed of desire, create the solid foundation. Once you have done this, you can rest assure when times get hard; they know where to go for comfort and guidance.

The second mistake I made was not recognizing that my son wasn't ready to be left alone. He wasn't ready to be living in the dorms without any structure. I was the one who woke him every morning when he was in high school. I cooked his meals and washed his clothes. He never even had a job to learn how to deal with responsibilities! Yes, I taught him how to be polite. How to make his bed and clean up after himself, I taught him how to be a gentleman and how to be respectful to his elders, but I hadn't taught him how to responsibly exist on his own. I didn't teach him how to manage his time, and I didn't teach him what the consequences would be if he didn't. I suppose I coddled him quite a bit. So, perhaps I shared in his failure. Of course, I did. I did the same with my daughter, and sadly, I didn't take heed. I was honestly quite caught up in my success as a mother that I wasn't paying attention to the small details. I didn't know it all when I was trying to raise my children. I was a single mother, and I was doing my best. I was motivated by my own adolescent failures, and all I could focus on was getting them across the high school graduation stage and into the doors of college. I thought the rest they could do themselves. They would learn along the way, as I did. Parents, let me tell you what I wish someone would have told me. Children need you far after they walk across that stage to receive their high school diploma. In fact, they need you to pay close attention to them in high school so that you can discern what the right path will be for them. Trust me, few high school graduates truly know. If you can, try to carve out time for daily undivided attention for your teenager. There is so much that we need to teach them that they don't learn in high school. There is also so much that we need to learn from them, like true comprehension of their own untouched desires. Desires that are not tainted with our wishes or hopes. I strongly suggest allowing your graduate a minimum one semester away from school before entering college. During that downtime, let them travel to a nearby city or state alone. Give them a tight budget and some tasks to complete along the way. Have them journal throughout the trip, capturing their emotions, identifying what was difficult, what was scary, what was exciting, and what they enjoyed most. Once they accomplish that task, give them another one, and another one. Give them a task that they will fail and teach them how to recover; give them their first adult lesson at resilience. If you are like me and you didn't prepare your child like you would have liked, let me tell you something, it's not too late to start over again. It may be a sticky situation in the beginning, but you can do it! The first step is to share in the blame of their failure. Of course, we are also at fault! If they are below twenty-three, they were still children in need of guidance. If you are not willing to share in the blame, renewing the relationship may be exceedingly difficult, or maybe even impossible.

Eventually, my son and I confessed and owned our contributions to his lack of success in college, and it was right in time. He was going through a really tough time with a sudden sickness that added to the depression he was already feeling, and he needed his mother. I considered it a blessing to be there to help him reset his life. My husband and I talked about it and decided to give him a few years of our dedicated attention. We wanted to take the opportunity to guide him through obtaining his associate's degree and help him establish a solid foundation before going out into the world again. When he returned home, we officially started over again; and we loved it!

The decision to start over with parenting my son brings us both closer to God. We were both holding on to negative feelings, which are sinful and against God. We learn in Leviticus 19:18 (NIV), "Do not seek revenge or bear a grudge against anyone among your people but love your neighbor as yourself. I am the LORD." It was such a relief to close that negative chapter and move in the direction of healing, love, and trust. It is too hurtful to imagine what life would have been separated from my son. If you have any animosity in your relationships, seek healing. Come together in forgiveness and love. Trust God and ask him to soften your hearts and pray that you will once again be blessed by each other's presence.

I have shared three of many start-over decisions that I have made in my life. I have also highlighted how all the disciples started over to follow Jesus. You may be thinking that your start-over situation is not the same as the ones I've shared. That it's just too hard to start over, or that you are not worthy of a second chance. I have often thought that, too, especially as it pertains to love. I used to think I wasn't worthy of true, unconditional love. I thought that I was too damaged to receive love and questioned whether or not I even gave it properly. I thought perhaps if I loved better, my significant other wouldn't have cheated, or friends that I considered precious wouldn't have disregarded me, or if I had loved better, I wouldn't have been physically abused, or that somehow, I had fallen out of God's grace, and wasn't fit for educational leadership any longer. It is not uncommon to question your worth when you have to start over. But keep two things in mind. The first is, we are typically at a low point if we need to start over, and when we are at that low point, we are most vulnerable to the devil's attacks. He will feed on your self-doubt. He will seize the opportunity to drag you down further to the pit of depression and despair, and he will be very convincing. So, know this, the second thing; you are worthy of starting over! God wants us to learn from our mistakes. He says our mistakes build perseverance; they build our patience and our faith. It requires us to call on Him for instruction and guidance; this is what he wants from us. He wants us to call on him, listen to his voice, believe, and obey. In the book of James says,

> Consider it pure joy, my brothers and sisters, whenever you face trials of many kinds, because you know that the testing of your faith produces perseverance. Let perseverance finish its work so that you may be mature and complete, not lacking anything. If any of you lacks wisdom, you should ask God, who gives generously to all without finding fault, and it will be given to you. [6] But when you ask, you must believe and not doubt, because the one who doubts is like a wave of the sea, blown and tossed by the wind.

James 1:2-8 (NIV)

So, trust me when I say it's okay to start over. In fact, we are incomplete until we go through trials and tribulations. Trials make us mature, make us strong, bring wisdom, and make us trust in the Lord. Believe in the Lord and repent your sins. He will bless you with the proper path for your new journey. If your start-over has nothing to do with sin or past mistakes, just believe with your whole heart that God has something better for you. Don't be afraid to let go of the present and have faith for what He has for you in the future; remember that in Jerimiah 29:1, God has plans to prosper you and not to harm you, but to bring you hope and a future.

Let's go back to the Bible for another example, an example of a woman who, according to the law, didn't deserve a chance to start over. When Jesus was teaching on Mount of Olives, he was presented with a woman caught in the act of adultery. The Law conveyed that a woman caught in the act of adultery should be stoned to death. But that wasn't Jesus' reaction at all. He didn't want to offer judgment nor see the woman harmed, even in her guilt. Isn't it evident that we serve a God of love and forgiveness? I believe this was such a beautiful moment in history, as I can clearly see God's intention here or what I believe his intention was. He used this as a teachable moment and a time of reflection for everyone in the crowd. Rather than judge the woman in front of her peers, he challenged the crowd, saying, if they were without sin, to cast the first stone at the woman. At that statement, all were convicted and slowly began to turn away because we all sin! His final response to the guilty woman was to go and leave your life of sin. Glory to God! She was indeed guilty, yet; He gave her a start-over. In fact, on that day, He may have given many people in the crowd an opportunity to start over. Please understand, you are worthy of another chance, and another, and another.

Whatever it takes! Jesus just wants you to sin no more. The Scripture reads,

> "Teacher, this woman was caught in the act of adultery. In the Law Moses commanded us to stone such women. Now what do you say?" They were using this question as a trap, in order to have a basis for accusing him. But Jesus bent down and started to write on the ground with his finger. When they kept on questioning him, he straightened up and said to them, "Let any one of you who is without sin be the first to throw a stone at her." Again he stooped down and wrote on the ground. At this, those who heard began to go away one at a time, the older ones first, until only Jesus was left, with the woman still standing there. Jesus straightened up and asked her, "Woman, where are they? Has no one condemned you?" "No one, sir," she said. "Then neither do I condemn you," Jesus declared. "Go now and leave your life of sin."

John 8:4-11 (NIV)

I would like to offer one more example to those who may still doubt. Perhaps you feel as though God was warning you time and time again, and you ignored his voice. Then one day, those warnings stopped, and you found yourself in a very unfortunate situation. You feel like your situation is the result of your disobedience to God. You may feel that the situation you are in is justified, that you deserve to suffer this obstacle. I am not one to tell you why you are in your situation, but I am one to tell you that our God is a forgiving God; so, don't lose hope. Set your heart right, and keep trying to stand up and start over, and in his time, he will grant you mercy and grace. Persevere. Let's take a look at King Nebuchadnezzar from the book of Daniel. He was a mighty ruler over the most magnificent land of his times. But he was a dishonorable man with a mean spirit and a cruel heart. He felt that his wealth and power came from his own doing. In fact, he even announces on his rooftop as he looked out over the magnificent city of Babylon, saying, "Look at Babylon, I built this great city!" He continues, saying that he built it to show how great he was. Now the crazy thing about this story was that sometime prior to his brief moment of self-exultation, the King had a disturbing dream about an enormous tree so large that it reached the heavens and could be seen by the whole earth. It had beautiful foliage, and it was fruitful, providing food for all. But the King couldn't interpret the dream. So, he sought someone who could explain it to him. The Prophet Daniel explained to the King that the tree was him, powerful and mighty. But Daniel tells the king that also in this dream, a holy messenger said to destroy the tree, tear it down, leaving only its stump and its roots in the ground, bound with a band of iron and brass around it, in the tender grass of the field. Let him be drenched with the dew of heaven and graze with the beasts of the field till seven times pass him by. The Prophet Daniel interpreted the mysterious dream. Explaining that the King was certainly the mighty tree but that he would be stripped of his power and driven to the fields to eat amongst the wild animals for seven years. He would basically lose his mind for seven years until he acknowledged that God is King of all. Daniel completed his interpretation with the advice that the King break away from sin and do what is right. The King, thankful for the interpretation of the dream, only focused on the first part of the dream, that he would be the most powerful and wealthy on earth. He paid little attention to the latter. So, fast-forward twelve months, there he stood on the rooftop declaring his glory. Before he could even finish his statement, a voice came from heaven and announced that his kingdom would be stripped from him and he would be driven away from his lovely Babylon to live in the fields with the animals for seven years. It happened immediately.

Even after being warned in the dream, King Nebuchadnezzar did his own thing and faced the wrath of God, losing his mind, and made to be on his hands and knees, living amongst the cattle in the field. But, remember in the dream, it said to leave the stump and roots in the ground; this was symbolic of Nebuchadnezzar returning to his kingdom after the seven years. The stump and roots were symbolic of his start-over after he declared that God was the one who blesses people with kingship, wealth, and power and that all Glory belongs to God. Nebuchadnezzar was blessed with a start over! The Scripture reads,

> At the same time my sanity was restored, my honor and splendor returned to me for the glory of my kingdom. My advisers and nobles sought me out, and I was restored to my throne, and surpassing greatness was added to me. Now I Nebuchadnezzar, praise and exalt and glorify the King of heaven, for all His works are true and all His ways are just. And He is

able to humble those who walk in pride.

Daniel 4:36-37 (NIV)

The story of Nebuchadnezzar is a prime example of God's grace and an opportunity to start over, regardless of our sins, and even when we ignore God's warning. Our God is so merciful ad good that none of us are unsavable.

Have you ever felt that you were unsavable? I have. Share your story here in the privacy of your book to get it off your heart and prepare yourself for a start over. _______

____

____

____

____

Think of a time when you had to start over, what did you learn from it? ______________________________

____

____

____

Is there a tug at your heart right now to let go of something? Is there something you need to relinquish, to perhaps make you available for something new? You will know because it will be a nagging feeling that has been tugging on you. What do you need to let go of? ________________

____

____

____

Remember in the last chapter we created a five-year

plan to grow, can you think of anything that may get in the way of your plans? Is there something that you need to conclude before you have clear access to accomplish your goals? What might be in your way, write it here. It's an obstacle that you must overcome in order to see your growth. If you don't name it, it may overshadow your success. Your first step to overcoming an obstacle is having the courage to identify it! ________________________________

____

____

____

____

Prayer

Dear Heavenly Father, God of chances,

Thank You for loving me so much that You allow me to start over in areas where I may have failed. Thank You for taking my moments of failure to allow me to grow. Thank You for allowing me to mature and gain wisdom by way of my failures. And Lord, in areas where I have not necessarily failed, but where I have maximized my time or potential and need a different challenge, thank You for bringing that path to a close, and pushing me to embrace a new direction. Lord, I know that You have a plan distinctly for me, and I also know that I am more inclined to follow the flesh, to follow my own desires and not seek You for direction, so thank You for closing the doors and making me weary, tired, and confused so that I must seek You for clarity. Lord, we often feel broken and defeated by our failures. We see starting over as a weakness, and Father sometimes we remain in a state of defeat, depression, and despair. Lord, remind us that we gain our strength in You, and open our eyes to the wonders and possibilities that lie ahead.

Lord, especially open our eyes to see that You are preparing us to fulfill the greatness that You have planned for us, Lord, that in our works, even though we may start over and over again, Lord, that ultimately Your mercy is seen in our life, and Lord, when we persevere and are triumphant, Lord, may all see that the Glory is Yours. Lord, we know that all success is Yours. Not just ours, but everyone's; and remind us often Father, You have a plan for this world, and that all things are working together for Your good. Lord, we love You, and we thank You for always being there for us, even as we start over again and again. In Jesus's name, Amen.

These are Scriptures that really speak to my spirit when it comes to starting over or for focusing on God's plan for my life. These Scriptures remind me that I am special, I am unique, and that God will never lead me astray. If I am tempted to go my own way, God will bring me back to him, even if that means closing doors and making me start over again. God will also equip me with the tools and knowledge I need to be successful in doing his work.

- Trust that God has a purpose for your life; read this Scripture to be reminded.

> Therefore, do not be anxious, saying, 'What shall we eat?' or 'What shall we drink?' or 'What shall we wear?' For the Gentiles seek after all these things, and your Heavenly Father knows that you need them all. But seek first the kingdom of God and his righteousness, and all these things will be added to you.

Matthew 6:31 (ESV)

- When it feels like you just can't go on, remember

God will not give you more than you can barely read this Scripture.

"No temptation has overtaken you that is not common to man. God is faithful, and he will not let you be tempted beyond your ability, but with the temptation he will also provide the way of escape, that you may be able to endure it" (1 Corinthians 10:13, ESV). Trust God as you fulfill his calling for your life. Read the three Scriptures below for reassurance.

> Now may the God of peace who brought again from the dead our LORD Jesus, the great shepherd of the sheep, by the blood of the eternal covenant, equip you with everything good that you may do his will, working in us that which is pleasing in his sight, through Jesus Christ, to whom be the glory forever and ever. Amen.

Hebrews 13:20-21 (ESV)

> "And I am sure of this, that he who began a good work in you will bring it to completion at the day of Jesus Christ".

Philippians 1:6 (ESV)

> I do not cease to give thanks for you, remembering you in my prayers, that the God of our LORD Jesus Christ, the Father of glory, may give you the Spirit of wisdom and of revelation in the knowledge of him, having the eyes of your hearts enlightened, that you may know what is the hope to which he has called you, what are the riches of his glorious inheritance in the saints.

Ephesians 1:16-18 (ESV)

KEY MESSAGE

I wish someone would have told me that starting over is not bad and that it should never carry a negative connotation in my life. In fact, it's just the opposite; it's freeing. Starting over is one of the main ways we learn in life; whether it's a list of spelling words, or a completely new career, starting over should be seen as uplifting and inspirational, not as a failure. In the moment, you may not feel inspired or uplifted, but if you look through the correct lenses, you will see the blessings and benefit in starting over. Every time we start over, we are learning to be resilient, and if we practice rational resilience, we will persevere. God says to consider it pure joy when trouble of any kind comes our way, knowing that it will build perseverance and give us an opportunity to grow and gain wisdom. Sometimes, if we are not made to hit rock bottom or experience some sort of catastrophe, we will remain in a situation that is not healthy for us, or we will remain stagnant, and we know that is not God's will for our life. God has a plan to prosper each and every one of His children. He has a calling or responsibility for all of us, and it may take starting over to take us closer to his plan for our life. I personally think that all my years in education have prepared me to be able to minister to you, to teach in a different way. But I wouldn't have ever taken this step on my own. I felt absolutely unworthy to share God's Word. I thought my insignificant little life couldn't possibly offer any lessons to others, but God told me otherwise. So, He created the space and opportunity for me to start over. As I mentioned in my other areas of starting over, I feel so much closer to God as a result of my restart; I've never felt closer. What about you? Have you ever hit rock bottom or experienced debilitating confusion and had to cry out to Jesus? Have you ever been at a loss for what to do and remained in an unhealthy state for a bit of time, finally receiving an opportunity to start over? Are you there now? If so, it's okay. You are exactly where you are supposed to be. Now, just go to God with the situation and seek His guidance. Try these words,

"Lord, I have hit rock bottom, or I just don't know where to go from here. Lord, I give up trying to find my way, Lord open my heart so that I may hear your still small voice guiding me to the correct path, Lord, I am ready and willing to follow, thank you, Lord, in advance for this victorious road you will lead me on, I believe. In Jesus' name, Amen."

Now you have to take the steps to get on that road. Then, you have to keep on moving in the right direction, one foot in front of the other. You have to keep on maturing, and sometimes that means you have to keep on starting over, but that's okay. Seek His guidance; start over again and again and again, because every time you do, you're getting closer to your calling, closer to God.

Epilogue

Every day is a new start. Every day we can choose to be better than we were the day before. In fact, we must! We must *intentionally* strive to be Christ-like. It is a characteristic we will never master, hence the intentional, never-ending effort. I literally have to be mindful of my actions, my words, my attitude, and my manner daily. I still struggle with my past, it steps in to haunt me every now and then, but now, I know how to overcome it when it happens.

We are not meant to forget the past; if we did, there wouldn't be such a thing as history. We are initially shaped by our past experiences, the good and the bad. But we are meant to learn from them and adjust our lives to ensure we don't make the same mistakes. It's okay if we take baby steps. It's okay if we have to start over again and again as long as we just keep moving forward. Starting over means growth. We are meant to grow and then to minister to those who come after us, saving them from some of the pain that we have experienced.

Do you know the best way to minister to others? It is to share your story. Share the hurts as well as the joys. Share how you have come to be the person you are today. Share what shaped your character from your childhood and past experiences. The biggest thing to share is to share how God has always been with you, even if, at times, you didn't realize it. Share that ultimately, it is only by the love, grace, and mercy of God, that you can share anything at all! He is the one who guides and protects; He is the one who gives strength. His is the only opinion that matters.

Share the Decision-Making Process. Tell the people you minister to not to go it alone. Tell them there is a solid foundation in which to make their decisions. Show them how to make goals and how to self-assess and strive to walk in the fruit of the spirit. Show them how to adopt positive character traits, and encourage them to look in the mirror and be able to describe themselves in three sentences! When I think about the impact we can have together by telling others what we wish someone would have told us, I get all giddy! If you don't think you are ready to minister to others, just share this book, and guess what? You will have ministered to someone that just may benefit from these messages.

May God bless you and guide you all the days of your life!

Bibliography

1. ScienceDaily. "Social isolation, loneliness could be greater threat to public health than obesity." Last modified August 5, 2017. www.sciencedaily.com/releases/2017/08/170805165319.htm

2. Bullying Statistics. "Bullying and Suicide." Accessed March 2, 2021. http://www.bullyingstatistics.org/content/bullying-and-suicide.html

3. Wasserman, D., Cheng, Q., & Jiang, G. X. "Global suicide rates among young people aged 15-19." *World Psychiatry, 4*(2), 114-120. (2005). https://ncbi.nlm.nih.gov/pmc/articles/pmc1414751

About the Author

Dr. Monique Kammer has been a leader in public education for most of her career, serving the educational system in the United States and abroad.

One day it was placed upon her heart that she would no longer be a leader of the typical academic curriculum, but a teacher of the curriculum of the Bible, God's Word, by sharing her own life stories, and testifying to God's glory, His mercy, and His grace.

Monique believes passionately that we can find Scripture, God's Word, to support every aspect of our lives, and if we just use it as the blueprint to life, we can reduce our suffering and increase our joy astronomically.

She is dedicated to touching as many lives as possible by sharing the joy, peace, and fulfillment that she receives from her Lord and Savior, Jesus Christ; a joy, peace, and fulfillment that she could never find elsewhere.

She is married to the love of her life and now resides in Las Vegas, Nevada.